Wakefield Libraries
& Information Services

This book should be returned by the last date stamped
above. You may renew the loan personally, by post or
telephone for a further period if the book is not required by
another reader.

NEW SELECTED POEMS

NEW SELECTED POEMS

1983–2008

John Fuller

Chatto & Windus

LONDON

Published by Chatto & Windus 2012

2 4 6 8 10 9 7 5 3 1

First published in Great Britain in 2012 by
Chatto & Windus
Random House, 20 Vauxhall Bridge Road,
London SW1V 2SA
www.randomhouse.co.uk

Addresses for companies within The Random House Group Limited
can be found at: www.randomhouse.co.uk/offices.htm

The Random House Group Limited Reg. No. 954009

A CIP catalogue record for this book
is available from the British Library

ISBN 9780701184322

The Random House Group Limited supports The Forest Stewardship
Council (FSC®), the leading international forest certification organisation.
Our books carrying the FSC label are printed on FSC® certified paper.
FSC is the only forest certification scheme endorsed by the leading
environmental organisations, including Greenpeace.
Our paper procurement policy can be found at
www.randomhouse.co.uk/environment

Typeset by Palimpsest Book Production Limited,
Falkirk, Stirlingshire
Printed and bound by CPI Group (UK) Ltd,
Croydon CR0 4YY

Contents

Author's Note

This new selection of my poems is drawn from the eight original volumes as listed in the Contents. Representing about twenty-five years' work between 1983 and 2008, it is intended as a sequel to my *Selected Poems 1954–1982*, which was drawn from the nine volumes published in the first twenty-eight years of my writing life. There is no overlap with that earlier selection, which is now out of print. As is the case with my *Collected Poems* (1996) I have not included any poems from volumes written for children, or in collaboration with others. Most writers look with less disfavour on recent work. They better remember the circumstances of its composition, and still, to a degree, feel responsible for it. I am therefore happy for this selection, the first general gathering of my work for more than fifteen years, to speak for me to new readers.

from THE GREY AMONG THE GREEN (1988)

Wednesday

Wednesday, black rabbit, seven years old,
You were silent all your short life as though
   Entrusted with a secret
   You could not be sure of keeping.

Easily startled, you would never turn your head
But stared in a still alarm through creepered brick
   Into that missing meadow
   Where danger would be a delight.

Not the eyes, a cloudy lidless brown,
But scissored ears positioned like microphones
   Brought the imaginary
   Misty horizons near.

Sometimes you dashed in joy from bed to bed
Like a comedian with surprises in the wings,
   Feet avoiding the fronds
   With a fastidious flick.

Not so many abortive burrows were yours
But the same one, not serious, under the rose.
   Your preferred occupations
   Were transporting paper

Or making circles around our wary heels
When on dewy evenings we trod
   With purpose or excuse
   Into your green domain.

Sturdy little president of the lawn!
We ignored your private moods; your gaiety
   Was at most a flourish
   In our casual moments

And when you were found, a stretched effigy,
A hard object so much like yourself
    But weirdly without motion
    And feared like an impostor,

The ensuing sorrow was the strangest thing,
A conscious grieving in a larger happiness
    That seemed designed to absorb
    Its choking negative.

Whatever strange lessons of death we learned
Touching your flat still body or pushing turf
    Into impromptu place
    Above the disturbed earth,

We prefer to make of you a remembered image
That accords with our myth of perpetual contentment,
    Of life as an unfolding
    Towards an unseen horizon.

And now at evening in the summer air,
With wine and fruit unfinished on the table,
    The candle sculpts a soft
    But meagre circle of shadows.

And as night comes, the garden is suddenly empty
Of a black shape in the blackness, coming from nowhere,
    Coming at an idle call
    Though never making a sound.

Breakfast

Mornings restore us to the physical
With the clink of familiar slight purpose,
Toying with a log-jam of All Bran
In milk almost blue, like a wrist.

The spoon has the weight and arched curve
Of a torso prepared for pleasure or pain,
Reminding us of dreams where we hunted
Free spirits down infinite spaces.

But the bowl, though endless, is finite,
A perfect white circle, with deceitful flowers,
A shape matched by the defining zones
Of our weakest spots: collar, belt.

Daughter

Once inside my head
The thought is hard to get out:
   Another daughter.

You were never ours.
Photographs showed you missing
   And no one noticed.

Intention was blind:
How near was your conception
   We shall never know.

The disqualified
Candidates can't believe the
   Office is unfilled.

You don't exist, but
Nobody can take your place:
   That space has been booked.

Three faces suggest
The fourth: compass points of the
   Parental axes.

Words like little loves
Presiding over a map
   For future journeys.

Prospero's secret
Sadness: I had peopled else
   This isle with daughters.

Only the subject
Of unuseful poetry:
   What never occurred.

Lawn Games

The rose shoots again
On its dead stump: there are things
    Not to be thought of.

Rambling blue flowers
Fade on the stone: bottle and glass
    Exchange their inches.

A heel on one knee,
A slight air cooling the sleeve:
    The eyes are restless.

Each grass blade aims high,
Each green corner joins arms with
    Its neighbour: a lawn.

Hoops turn the lawn to
A lucky six: the sun looks
    Down on a red ball.

Palace of pleasures:
Beauty is ignorant of
    Being imagined.

Five doves on the lawn:
Celestial fingerprint,
    A kiss from earth's lips.

Nape, elbow, instep:
Her rug settles after a
    Smooth flight from Turkey.

Ten toes, heels lifted:
Ankle bones like buds of wings,
    Eyes shut to the sky.

Lucy's Daffodil

Poorly finger, it didn't know
What it was doing. Now cut in water
It preaches from the tumbril of spring
A last speech on survival. It leans
Into a mysterious angle of beckoning
As if for inspection or attention,
Turning all sound green.

Chill flower, its ribbon pumped
With air, one jewel on the stem
Like a lost bathysphere,
It reaches from the rattling window as if
Hammered from what little light
Winter has admitted, scared
To be reclaimed by the wind.

Tissue lifts from the stalk knuckle.
The baby bell is haunted, nowhere
Else to turn. Its silent yell
Is like a gasp for oxygen
Claiming the whole room in the name
Of an emotion still to be invented.
What does the sun say? I can't hear.

Avoid Contact with the Eyes

You are safe here, in a protective envelope
That stays the shape of your body, warmer than blood,
A horizontal cubicle with a levitated
Door of water, a flooded sarcophagus
To revive in, anointed. If you cut the cord
The life will leak away again. If you sing
Someone will rush in, pretending alarm,
To see for one steamy moment two big eyes
And meringue hair. He will rush out again
For fear of being involved in your inviolable
Voyage and its exciting but innocent islands,
For though in that amused instant you lie
As still as art or geology, there on the edge
He will see the dangerous potion in sudden close-up
And the instructions are quite clear on the bottle.

Synopsis for a German Novella

The Doctor is glimpsed among his mulberry trees.
The dark fruits disfigure the sward like contusions.
He is at once aloof, timid, intolerant
Of all banalities of village life,
And yet is stupefied by loneliness.

Continually he dreams of the company he craves for,
But he challenges it and bores it to tears whenever
It swims uncertainly into his narrow orbit.
Meetings, however relished in their prospect,
Seem only to be arrangements for departures.

Exemplum: the spruce Captain and his vampire wife
With her token fur hat and veil, like a bandage
Extemporised by a bat. It seems that exercise
Keeps the Captain's horse in a permanent lather.
The wife suffers from a disabling ennui.

What more likely than a harmless liaison?
At their first meeting the scenario is as obvious
As a cheese. Her eyes, half-lidded, turn away,
The cup lifted to her lips. The Captain has questions
About the flooding of the water-meadow.

A furious but undirected energy governs her soul,
Listless as she seems on the surface. It is
A libido on auto-destruct. Opportunities
Occur, but the Doctor, in complacent rectitude,
Bows himself off the stage of further meetings.

He devotes himself to his patients. They, however,
Begin to avoid him as if he has some dreadful disease.
When the Captain is lost on the glacier, his horse
Riderless, returning to graze on the bowling-green,
The Doctor is suspected. It is most unfair.

Meanwhile, his orphaned cousins go ahead
With their threatened law-suit. At first he is amused.
He meets their legal representative over
A schnapps in the Bahnhof Buffet, and is compromised
By the leather luggage of the absconding wife.

He claims to have found a cure for the epidemic of goitres
But only succeeds in killing two maids and a barley farmer.
The Captain's wife is staying at Interlaken
With the Schoolmaster's wastrel son. Her insane letters
Are read out in court, evidence of the Doctor's malpractice.

Only his good old Nurse refuses to disbelieve him.
On her death-bed she grips his fingers tightly
And mutters inaudibly about the lost diaries.
There is nothing now to prevent the red-haired cousins
From taking complete control of his estate.

The Doctor has lost everything and gained nothing.
At the back of his mind there is still the slight hope
That time will explain to him his crucial role.
He becomes a cutter of peat, and realises
That it is never quite easy enough to disappear.

Eyes and Lips

Reading the lesson of the eyes
And paragraphs of lips,
Hands need only touch the face
As if to keep their place

And eyes have nothing at all to do
But speak to other eyes,
And lips absorb their own reflection
Without objection.

Eyes move guiltily, uncertain
Of their coordinates.
Lips receive distinct impressions
In lengthy sessions.

These faculties communicate
With freely borrowed roles
When the whole skin surface goes walking,
Good looking, small talking.

But then, as if such paradoxes
Were not enough, consider:
All this was simply what eyes did.
This was what lips said.

The Visitor

How can I begin?
And who will let me in?
I lean upon the far side of your mind
As if a door could learn
It had a hinge to turn
And, opening, disclose what was behind.
I whisper the appealing word
You claim you do not wish to hear, but surely heard.

Windows, as windows must,
Yawn on their jaws of rust.
Their catches snap, their webs are stretched and broken.
Curtains on their rings
Stretch like the folded wings
Of some dark-lidded bird too soon awoken,
For whom a gently sleeping wood
Makes restless sounds that it would fathom if it could.

And now a little air
Stirs in the rafters where
Tied sprays of leaves and herbs are slowly turning.
It wakes the drowsy fire
And makes the flames leap higher
To tell the silent room that they are burning.
It corners rugs with its embrace
As though by folding down a page to mark its place.

You find me in the gloom
Of the chill morning room
Before the fire is stirred or curtains drawn,
And through the ticking day
As hours slip away
I shadow small things struggling to be born.
I am the chimney and the mouse
And all the little noises of the midnight house.

The cat before the coals
From which the smoke in scrolls
Describes the movements of the massy air
Knows that I'm inside
And have a place to hide,
Although her blinking will not tell her where
And motionless her paws lie curled
About the dreaming suburbs of her tabby world.

On and about I go,
Carefully to and fro,
To keep the bedclothes you threw back in tangles.
Silently I explore
Your papers on the floor,
Arrange the furniture at curious angles
In rooms to which you are returning
To find a pan still simmering or lamp still burning.

And now you are aware
That I am living where
You notice these familiar surfaces,
And though I am unseen
You know where I have been
And understand what secret motive is
By now implicit in that being,
Impelling you to this necessity of seeing.

I am the secret print
Of fire within the flint.
I am the sleeping spark that dreams of tinder.
I am the wood that sings.
I am the tongue that springs
To sudden life upon the dying cinder.
I am the burning in your eye
That sets the world alight and will not let it die.

Swimming at Night

Swimmers intend to be born again. Their laughter
And purpose bespeak a creature of consciousness

Even when descending a mad path to the night sea,
Stumbling at a damp curtain of black air

When the blackness itself has secret shades of black:
Purse black, space black, the black over the shoulder.

The eye that has no need to see looks nowhere,
But hands reach out for the bond of touch

Whose intention is some sort of commitment to the
    elements,
Linked and cautious on the delirious gradient,

Elements which perform their nuptials like a great drama
Proving an expressive bond of contraries:

Clouds heavy with the charge of a ready storm
Bounce their energy from the fused ceiling of air.

Thunder in a flickering jumble of light in the hills
Exposes the sea's swirling danger and glamour

And the damp is distinguished as an insistent fine rain
That joins sky and tide in drifts of forgetting.

This is a ritual where nothing was known beforehand,
Urged by the meteorological preamble.

Pleasures must be insignificant beside the attention
Of like to like, salt blood, salt water.

Clothes are bundled from the drizzle, a stub
Of candle flickering in the dredged hulk,

A dead boat beached in the invisible sand
That dwindles, though groined and lantern-steady,

Tiny along the shore as blackness reassumes
The crawling skin like a vestment.

And now hands break the sea as thunder breaks again,
And diving shocks the depths to a response:

Turbid with lit plankton like spokes and clocks,
The salt galaxies are bruised into being by our bodies.

Little fitful beacons of dull watery light
Sharpening the dark as the gallons glop about us

And the air splits and cracks and the rain falls
Alive on the blind surface of the sea.

It was not what we intended. It is not us.
It is something quite other. It is the first thing.

This strange submarine light is a hoarded scattering
Like the earliest seeds, like the touch of kisses.

It is damaged stars, like blotted lightning,
Like points to be joined that would give us wings.

Being born is a gasping and drenching.
It is cold and clean as the dead centre of night.

We have no thought of returning,
Consciousness switched off at the source.

Reckless of gravity, the candle lost,
We strike in light and darkness from the shore.

Past

The wind is never freer
From having hair to blow
When we have left the mountain
Before the early snow.

The grass can grow no taller
Beneath our absent tread
And flowers are never wasted
When all the flowers are dead.

The night comes as it has to.
The moon and Wilbur kiss.
With no one there to see it,
What memories will we miss?

The seasons have no hunger
To please us with their sport,
And only words as restless
Betray what we have thought.

And even those emotions,
From being once exposed,
Are like the closing chapters
Of books forever closed.

Goodbye

One by one they say goodbye.
The plans and promises, like sky,
Are for the moment perfectly clear,
But wait till tomorrow:

A little cloud no bigger than
The parting handshake of a man
Who promises he will be back
Thins on the zenith

And there above the roofscape drift
The gloomy greys that never lift
On friends who calculate their hope
In single figures.

Their lips meet like equations of
Elaborate formulae of love
Which founder on some trivial error
And won't come right.

And so they draw away, unequal.
A gradual goodbye's the sequel
Of yet another episode
That came to nothing.

You are the one who's left behind
And tell yourself you must not mind.
You are the hub of all dispersals
But where does it leave you?

Goodbyes like particles define
Their centre with a random line
That only points back to a past
Hypothesised.

And that event becomes your whole
Existence. It is like a role
That keeps you waiting in the wings
For something to happen.

The play itself, although you wrote it,
Would need another life to float it.
The dialogue is dust, the curtain
Not rising or falling.

Yes, these are the goodbye years,
As though the second of three cheers
Has caught the guests with glasses raised
But horribly empty.

The smiles are fixed upon their faces,
The printed names in all the places,
Someone hands flowers, the cameras flash,
But no one is looking.

You've got just one more red to pot.
You've got to make that crucial shot.
You move up to the table, ready
To take all the colours

And when you see the ivory fall,
A futile trickle of your ball
Leaves you tucked in behind the black,
Lost to the yellow.

As, high and dry on narrowing land
You look about your spit of sand
To see who cares to take the odds
And share it with you,

And what you find is rising tide,
The sun gone down, nowhere to hide
And birds that gather in the air,
Dismally calling.

Yes, this is the time that kills.
The losing shot. The empty skills.
And the wild sense of saying so,
Over and over.

from THE MECHANICAL BODY (1991)

The Mechanical Body

Lifting a curl of its hair mounted on gauze,
Inserting the key into one ear oiled with its own wax,

You were at first surprised by its yielding and weight,
The way you could wind it to a pitch of response.

The whole mass trembled with released springs,
A shuddering at the heart of it like laughter.

It stunned the player with its fringed opening eyes,
Making the onlookers instinctively draw back.

But it was all surface and expedient dollwork,
With hidey-holes for soul and coils for motive.

Unfinished the canyon of the stitched chest,
The mirror fragments, the panels of easy access,

The lacunae (. . .) (. . .) behind the knees,
The temporary leather, the hinged armpits,

Stencilled flowers on the linen ribs,
Your hands disappearing into glue.

Its sentiments worked on pulleys and punched rolls,
Tinny between bellows and horn-membrane.

The first hummings and trillings eased into
A pert sotto chirrup: 'Now then, Bertie!'

Little fans spun above the turning cylinders
And, with a tilt of the whirring chin and a slight click,

'Do it again, do it again, do it again' modulated
Into deeper more thrilling pronouncements,

And whatever you cared to say came flatteringly back
From a library of teeth shining and uplifted

As the vibrations in the throat sang out their triumph
Of elocution: 'Tonight – cherry tart!'

That face was all-important, the ivory jaw
Traced in one chisel-sweep from lobe to lobe,

The nose a guardian of resonance, vellum temples,
The powdered cheeks borrowed from mandarin hangings,

Best was the mouth, embroidered minutely,
Hidden the hooks and wires that trembled it into motion.

Their working went deep into the busy centre
Of emptiness, as from the flies of a theatre:

Oiled strands trundled from a central gear
Slung between the rolling pivots of the hips.

The sounding vibrato of the belly concealed
The whine of its continual working.

Its long strings leading to that simple ring
Through which they fanned, the ring contracted

And its webs and skeins diversified into
A pursed amusement or a moue of disgust

Or turned inside-out like a cat's-cradle,
Offering its watered-silk tapestry for kisses.

How the onlookers cheered! The thing was rooted,
Statuesque, a third larger than life.

It was gaunt with dust and tulle.
Bits of it glittered, even in the dark.

Great springs slowly lifted the padded knees,
Whiskery skirts leaking oil on to the floorboards.

And all the time was this ripple of felt and enamel,
This little jabbering of hammers and pulleys:

Its talking might talk you through till morning.
Your back was bruised from its attentions.

You thought of figureheads and oceans.
You thought of young mothers in their milk.

You thought of the egg-smooth backs of eyeballs
Staring unknowingly into the smoky caves of the future.

You thought of your life as a cheerful wager,
As a torn ticket of entry, a key to be used once.

You thought of cog turning cog turning cog,
The perpetual motion of the Last Chance.

You thought of the questioning of beauty in eternity,
Your hands at the controls, and celestial signs.

But as it wound down, its fingers barely twitching,
A tell-tale ticking from the ratchets of its joints,

There was nothing in the business but a blush,
A scattering of applause, a stillness.

And in that stillness, the postscript of a last
Creaking inch of clockwork was like a hollow laugh:

Hollow as the likeness of truth to a skull.
Hollow as the starlight pull of the doll.

Silhouettes

Sister, when I saw your toe whiten
Beneath the blade I thought it was already
Parted from pain and ready to be pitied.
I thought the business done, detached for ever,
Drained of the salt source we share, mere lump.
But that was only fear. The thing was still
Alive, though tensed and bent, like a small man
Almost used to being hurt, the arms
Clasped over the head, flinching from words.
And the scissors, for a moment, still had the skin
To cut. And, look! your hand still held the scissors.
Who said we had to be the shapes we are?
Or that those shapes are not desirable?

Sometimes in the lamplight I could think
Myself not more than shadow-deep from beauty.
Noses and chins on walls are graced a little
And get on terms. I could hug anyone
And never feel ashamed, or if refused
Refused with interest, fondness or respect.
Just a little does it. Like a cabbage:
Each leaf of such a thinness as you strip
To the heart, but that small centre is soon reached.
I think that everyone has once at least
Woken and wept themselves to sleep upon
A restless bed, alone and half an inch
From being hideous. Much more then, we.

When I heard your intake of breath, and the low
Growl of pain from your throat, I knew it was done,
Though cleverly you concealed that new object,
That part of you so like a grave of itself
With its grey little tombstone of a nail.
And you walked so proudly before the prince

26

As if in glory, with a baleful knowing enticement,
A smouldering glower as if bearing down on his mouth
With your determined mouth, and a small swagger
As without limping you placed each foot on the tightrope
Of the flagstones and no one to notice the slight
Leak at the gripping apron of the slipper.
O sister, though envious, how I prayed for you!

To fail is to want followers. But I
Was by your side, as sisters always are.
I took the scissors and put them in my sleeve.
(Were you to keep what you had seemed to win,
I knew that there was evidence to hide.)
It was not love, nor being a bride of blood.
It was not kingdoms, but a kind of justice.
For there was a fairy creature at the dance
Revolving by the beat, her skirts aflame.
The orchestra was hers, and hers the pulse
Of the night's bodily music, and the stars
Came out for her and for her tiny feet,
And I was wholly with you in revenge.

She took the perfect hours her shape allowed her,
But that was all. The truth has times that are
Unwilling servants of their wilful master
And if she changed her shape again, who knows
What spate of goblin nuzzlings might ensue?
Just once she could be goggled at for being
All she might ever want to be. The rest,
The future beyond the hours, the hours beyond
The future, are nothing but a demi-mask:
Blank as to insight, but cut out for speaking
As speaking is the staying of those hours.
Behind it is the dark we always face,
And silhouettes a dangerous game with scissors.

Now is my time. The crystal slipper wiped
And once again presented on its cushion.
The ceremony is a dream repeated,
Our whole life winding down, a second chance,
The last and only chance, the lifted mask.
What do I risk? I shall go down again
Into the hall with perfect staircase paces.
It might be nothing more than a raw place
At the heel, a scouring, a deliberate blister.
We lose such linings by the moon. A triumph!
For after all I am the elder. It is
Fitting. I am called. My foot is treading
For ever in its liquid sock of skin.

Photograph

The image of a possession, possessing and being
Possessed by a mystery, stares from this face,
One finger at the cheek, the eyes searching.
There is a double distance: hypothetical
Space, our space; and the studio's.

Light blinked into the brass and guarded chamber:
A faint perception of the curious way that
Something rehearsed could still be unexpected
Showed in the equal distance of her mouth
From either recognition or repose.

It might be almost words about to break
Out there, a smile's postponement of itself
In puzzlement, amusement half-dispelled,
Before the settling of the lips in trust
That ceremony is a silent thing.

And we have nothing but our privilege
To share this silence and its lineaments:
Low forehead, heavy brow and rueful chin,
Young as if for ever and the leasehold
Of its occasion's awkward fragile beauty.

She was not often much like this and now
Can never be again, but over and over
Looks through and at us from the knowledge that
This mystery has thought to touch her with,
A face outfacing all its history.

What has just passed is like the tree above
Her grave where birds shrilly debate their
Breaking from the clamour that they make, until
They burst from leaves and flock about the sky.
The moment afterwards is still to come.

Masks

One brumy night in early November when cheeks
Were cold to kiss and mist all loose in the grove
At the height of a coffee-table or a craven Jack Russell
So that you could not think of running there
Without dog-slobber or barked shins or simply having
Mysteriously missed your legs in the flooded field
We came back panting and laughing to a book-lined world

And you knelt on the rag-rug in your chimneyless room
Till the gas-fire played steadily like a small
Ceramic organ, the curtains not quite drawn.
It was at that moment when you reached for me, your hands
At my waist like an iris vase too heavy to hold,
Worth the admiring and nowhere to put it down,
That I stiffened and put one finger to your lips.

'Not now!' I was suddenly unreasonably distracted
By the thought of an expressionless face staring in
Like a guy, like the window's misty breathed mask
But without breath, the mouth and eyes mere slits,
Like a hooded face, both torturer and victim.
I said: 'If we pay him will he go away?'
But you said there was no one and you looked severe.

I couldn't keep up my appeal to this admonitory
Absence, or appease a self-induced scare
As though it were an eager High Street drunk
Stiff with dried spillings and a crooked smile
Leaning from the wall: 'Miss, a word with you!'
An old guy, who smelled of need and sorrow,
Sad adult, little father, burned father!

When you poured two tiny gins I was aghast
At the mockery of that painted mask's beseeching.
'Make it three!' But your lips smiled and tightened
In a weary ironical grimace and you tidied

The curtains' corners like a cloth on an invalid's tray.
You had seen real faces staring in – as so often
You stared, serene in thinking, stonily back.

Perhaps the face was your own reflection or
The result of a longing of mine too often repressed.
As the evening lengthened our eyes no longer met
At the explosions and my thoughts survived their puzzlement
As they lifted brightly up the chimney of the dark,
So many brave little wayward twinkling smuts
Skittering in smoke towards the hanging moon.

Off the Record

Three months to clear the creeper, twined about them
Thigh-thick in places, the amorous grasp of nature:

Pedestals in slime, and obelisks,
Great bevelled diadems and shafts, worn domes.

Most were tiered, sky-reaching, monumental.
Some lay tilted, overturned like idols.

Playthings of the gods, we called them, towers
Stubborned with iron, beasts and pinnacles.

Stone carved into frond-shapes that the skin feels
Inside it, stone blood or nostril, stone like sand.

Stone carved into space-shapes that the sun makes
On eyelids, stone shell or earlobe, stone like pearl.

So intricately carved that, when we hacked,
Nestlings escaped in fright like clouds of spice.

From one, tugging at tendrils we were surprised
By dripping from its lip a muttering of monkeys.

To civilise, that is our mission's purpose.
We have a name for everything we do.

Yet that deep vale now shorn of vegetation
Seemed more especially immensely sad,

A place designed for some forgotten purpose,
A place of energies, of interruption,

A place of understanding and of struggle,
A place of blank unusual namelessness.

Years in that dismal cirque, with knotted ropes
Charting relationships and distances.

We crushed new ink, and in the Record wrote
The names we gave, recording their positions:

Red: Empress, Cardinal, Rhinoceros,
Talia, Talia, Cardinal and Terror.

White: Elephant, Dabbaba, Concubine,
Talia, Champion, Talia and Terror.

Red: Mann, Mann, Mann, Giraffe and Mann.
White: Empress, Rhinoceros and Cardinal.

From the surrounding peaks (three miles of steep
Ascent) we saw much less, but saw more clearly,

Saw that position was relationship,
That space was time, and form a form of power.

This may be done to that, and that to this,
And something else, though not the first, to that.

The Record taught us so: volumes of love,
Of growth and illness, itemised in codes.

We have a name for everything we do.
We have a code which tells us how it's done.

But what of codes for that strange architecture?
Balm for its captures, charms for its every move?

Without impelling touch it was itself
A code: we knew there were no codes for codes.

Rules for this god-game would describe itself,
Itself be understood outside all codes.

No reference to wrestling grips, the shrill
Cries of the breathless, or the stop of blood.

No round Os of surprise, the failure of
Attention, the missed opportunity.

No slackening of attack, the vertigo
Of daring irreversible decisions.

No sensations down the skin, collapse
Of knees, surrender of all tender surface.

From that pure height the pillars still outfaced
The morning mists and our interpretations.

After a week, forced to descend for water,
We closed the Record, all intent abandoned.

Of neighbouring tribes, flushed from the dwindled jungle,
There was nothing for the Record, little to say.

For some of us (too tired now to return
To fame, or bargaining with emeralds)

There was the prospect of a sluttish future
With their squat stolen daughters, who knew some tricks,

Peering between their legs as if to frighten
Wolves, their smiles turned into hideous groans

And sinewy honey-extracting tongues, so long
The tip could touch their anus like a wand.

Their language was a babble much like any,
With twenty different words for roasted oyster.

They said it used to be a paradise,
But we've no skill to make it so again.

Staring from wormy verandahs at the night,
We only note the creeper's slow advance,

Note pulsing in the neck, cries in the dark,
The sense of life as an unwilled postponement,

Note toothlessness, the monkeys come again,
And tendrils round the bases of those stones.

Unanswered questions: if they belonged to gods,
Then were they left behind through carelessness?

Or were the gods surprised? If so, by whom?
If a deliberate bequest, what then?

What could that war of white and red portend
And what its long unknown abandonment?

Gifts that we cannot handle may be stowed
Somewhere, but these we live beneath, like laws.

To civilise! Indeed. And then to dream
Of paradise, dream of the absent gods!

Perhaps these dreams are what we should preserve,
A way to write, and keep, the code of codes.

Otherwise I shall simply die like this,
Naming the millionth star then turning round

To creep from the verandah to the bed,
There to make love, and other useless games.

Bog

Kneeling for marshfruit like spilled
Beads bedded in displaying moss
I notice a licked frog dragging
His drenched fatigues up and through
The barring spears and stalks of orange
Bog asphodel as if in terror
Of unknown purposes, as though
I were a weight of sky, a whole
Universe of beak and gullet,
And not, as I am, a mere slider
And stumbler like him, damp to the hips,
Reaching for tussocks, scrabbling for almost
Nothing: these little speckled fruits,
Chill marbles of a forgotten tourney,
Aching playthings of a lost garden
That has always been mostly water,
A place of utter loneliness,
Terrain of the asphodel and of the frog.

Stony Acres

Something is gaping like a broken wall
In vacant fields. It must be the heart's spillage.
Yes, they've been down and up and down before,
These stones. This fresh collapse will take some clearing:
Migrant pieces needing to be flung back
In flinty protest; muddy chunks, and broken
Trapezoid wedges broadening to the shape
Of plates or blade-bones; wandering boulders; hopeful
Lintels whose weathered foreheads show how once
They coped; hurt shale; careless pebbles dancing
Dark down the hollowness inside; and some
Half-buried in the grass like plinths or armour
From fateful battles, immense in ancient moss.
Stemming this sprawl becomes a timely lesson:
A wall in place may be, like self-esteem,
A discipline of the damaged heart, yet somehow
With nothing much in sight that could escape
Or wander freely in, this dogged keeping
Of well-known lines and formal boundaries
Seems nothing better than an idle pleasure,
Balancing, wedging, stowing every crack
To cast long shadows on these stony acres.

The Two Teapots

The small teapot to the large teapot,
Stewed as a pond: 'When you last spoke,
Chuckling generously from your girth and glaze,
There were many who listened, who were friends.
Where are they now?'

The large teapot to the small teapot,
Clogged to a trickle: 'Peace, brother,
Your words are still warm and waited-for
By one who will be loved, though alone.
Be contented.'

Eating the Still Life

The wind is in the stove tonight and we
Must not eat the still life. A shuddering
Passes across the chimney. The coals glow.

We made this civil practised silence out of
Thought that dwells on shapes. We know we must
Not eat the still life. Eyes look down and up.

The stove is booming like a basset-horn.
Apples in the basket glow. We know
We must not eat the still life. We draw.

We make these ceremonious shapes in silence
That lives in thought. We know we must not eat
The still life. Beauty is a translation.

Its burning rises into the night. Are these
Apples or faces that we draw? The fire
Leaps, and we must not eat the still life.

At Sunset

The fear of everything, the fear
Even to name fear, a kind of content
To sit in the spreading light, to sit
Helpless like an exhausted mother at last,
Amused and perplexed at our most precious gift,
Sitting and watching it go.

No, the feeling is like a child's,
In fact is a child, waiting for a word,
The word that comes at the end of a long day,
At the end of all its ragging and play.

What word is it? Who knows?
Something between rest and a kept promise
All the more valued for the keeping,
Known long since and only half-resisted.

As on this very evening, noticing
Such a weird light against the wall:
Forgotten whatever I looked up from,
Forgotten the fatigue, forgotten the fear,
Forgotten in this sense of possession and stillness,
The stream loud after a recent rain
And the sun leaking like fire beneath the door.

Tree Fungus

Standing to attention by the wall that once divided
Cottage-ground from field-bits and the beginning
Of steep descent to a rabble of civilian oaks,
It never questioned or guessed what it might have guarded
But grew in girth, eased stones aside, spread boughs.

A gate-place disappeared and corners collapsed.
The wall was nothing much, for what was on one side
Knew it could just as easily be on the other,
And what sheep started continued with digging for buttons
And roots growing through bottles in that littered ground.

Already the ash wore its medals of lichen with pride
And round its base in October the tell-tale signs
Of superannuating *Pholiota squarrosa* clustered,
Yellow pixie fringes sprouting at its coat,
Little insistent fingers probing its weakness.

Then winter, signing off the year with its flourishes
Of slate-slithering wind, delivered its stroke
And the great shape hit the deck in a dead
Faint, thought by many to be its last,
Hinged from its roots in gaping mountainous splinters.

But still it lived, sap flooding through the flap
To send up spindly shoots at what were really
Downward angles from the recumbent trunk,
While the still-sprouting crown, disguised in grass
Offered unusual food to inquisitive sheep.

It couldn't last for ever, this suspended state,
Reduced in leaf-lift and soil-suction, in all
Standing and buoyancy that makes a tree.
Branches that tangled with cables had to be sawn,
Its stumps leaked, its whole scope was diminished.

Well, it is our fate to live with symbols
For just so long as we ourselves persist,
Old soldiers of the paced life, admiring
Old soldierly qualities wherever we find them,
Hoping for nothing beyond the daily horizon.

So when, as ever in April, once more this year
Its buds blacken at the tips of its stretched fingers,
We are pleased to stand on its collapsed shoulders
And stroke its wild clumsy arms with a touch
That intends encouragement, a calming of terror.

It is then that we notice a new growth, the invader,
Daldinia concentrica appearing at the wrists
And pulse-spots in a lavish globular blistering,
Smooth exuded bulges running into each other,
Of a mineral hardness and coppery invalid brown.

Is this to be seen perhaps as a kindly harbouring
Of a vagrant fruit-body by one with weakened resistance?
Or is it pure power, an edging-out of the host?
It's a fungus not seen before, not edible, not lovable,
But whatever a tree does it is still a tree.

Hope and Hearts

In the brown garden
Where playing lost its shadow
Among the lonely trees

These pale children of November
Rise from leaves
To forbid the frost and burning.

Frilfralog round the oaks
Tipsy and teetering
Putting up parasols

Skirted and stiff as dolls,
Never so still a dance,
So haunted a step

Till limp they lie down
Spilling their frills
In a lavish sprawl.

Everything goes back to earth
But first it must dance,
Dance to exhaustion.

They are our strangest thoughts,
Music of a mood
That will always create them

A solemn raggedy dance
At the year's end
But still as our own games

Games of outlandish endeavour
Games of promising
Games of hope and hearts

And like their rules
Allowing all they allow
And sometimes unbroken.

from STONES AND FIRES (1996)

History

In memory of Angus Macintyre

Then came the frost to put its signature
Upon the earth, tight and white as a knuckle
Above a contract that yields whatever is owed
But long before its time, and every creeper
And every blade of grass stood halted and still
As if by some spell that kept them from their growing,
Suspended in the cold ghosts of what they had been,
Preserved for a future that no one could guess.

The miniature angel blowing its gold trombone
Like an unfolded paper-clip announced
The matters arising, that whatever we had expected
Was now to be reviewed, a matter for silence,
Life postponed for this session, a halted process.
Whatever the coloured stars and eggs proposed
Referred back to a body that was powerless
For once to put the idea into effect.

A man is carrying a piece of wood
Like furniture, but to be hurt with it.
These stories, when we think of them, still shock,
Though never as much as all that is not story,
Conditions of being, the general state of things,
Information received, the bald facts,
Experience as it stupidly shoulders past us:
No wonder we have to make such stories of it.

Something at the best of times has almost
Believed in us. It is, like an only child,
The outcome of our passions, and so we tell it
What otherwise we might ourselves forget
Or could never defend unless called to account
By its wide-eyed searching gaze, its absolute
Faith in our own accountability,
Our fear of inheriting an alien world.

And it is always past, before we can know it.
Just as our individual lives, which we see
In daunting or luring prospect, minute by minute,
Make little sense until we are seen by others
As completed fact or anecdote, not likely
To slip out of character, palpably there.
Is this, then, our chance of eternity?
And what would you, what can you, say of it now?

I see you walking gravely through the mist
In the gangster hat and the oiled fisherman's jacket,
Passing the deer with their ignorance of history;
Passing that monument whose yearly ruin
Is a sign of its treasured leafage and renewal,
With its aching shoulders propped in lavish repose;
Passing to that north-eastern corner of Cloisters
Where the young Addison pondered the stoic of Utica.

And pondering yourself the puzzle of how we come
Through all the undetonated chances and mistakes,
Following the mothballed flag of our assumptions,
To this Janus-knowledge of our future and duties,
Of what we must say that is just, and what we should do,
What kind of story we make of the present moment
As without any excuses it simply buggers off.
The right way to proceed, as you always put it.

And I see you presiding over the account
Which history gives of our provisional forgiveness.
Reaching your room, you motion me to a chair,
That ancient leather into which your pupils sank
Gratefully, as into their understanding,
And you take two glasses, and a friendly bottle,
For this is now a dream, or is the spirit
Of the once that tells us who we are.

It tells us twice, two sides of the flipped coin:
It is the once of the unique, the once-only,
The once of happening, of not to be repeated;

It is also the once of the past, the once of then,
The once of story, the once of all that is lost.
It gives us everything, but takes it away.
It says: 'This is for now, and hardly to be imagined.'
It says: 'This has been revealed, but never again.'

I drink to you. In turn you raise your glass.
And all that we have to decide in this quiet place
Must still obtain your approval: 'I think that's right.'
'I think that must be the right way to proceed.'
The gravity of your tone is achieved through full
Consideration of all that might disturb:
The haunting thought of failure, the slight mistake
That would instantly reverse the entire intention.

Or sometimes, with your mouth's severe compression
Giving a dramatic emphasis to some
Fully imagined but quite insane prospect:
'We simply can't allow that to happen. Ever.'
Underlining, as you did, with a sudden gleam
Of the eyes, the solemnity of the prohibition,
An awful warning made the more chastening
By the brief ensuing twinkle of a smile.

For you realised, too, the infinite comedy
Of muddle and pride, the occluded puddle of theory.
At the slightest conceit or duff solemnity
Your knees sagged, your elbows concertinaed,
Finger jabbing the invisible victim in glee.
Your laughter celebrated the melting of rectitude.
It was a defence against the grim obsessions
That fuelled the Preacher, or the Flame-Haired Temptress.

It was also a love of the half- or the wholly innocent,
Sympathy for the feckless, a trust in the survival
Of the amiable, the outlandish, the incorrigible.
A disbelief, though without faltering, in the sheer
Presumption of begetting, of passing muster,
Of taking everything on without complaint.

Of our follies as young fathers, of the fallibility
Of senior counsel. It was Bertie's mauve shirts.

How often when you drove up England's spine
Had I taken the other, shoulder road which ended
In the ambiguous rocky arm of Wales,
Forbidding Ireland, or perhaps escrying her,
Or even holding out a hand in welcome.
We left behind our unbiological lives,
We left what is agreed for the agreeable,
We left the shorter for the longer view.

We shared these acres, glosses on pastoral texts
Where civility to survive must prove a truth
Plainer than law and friendlier than estates,
Where the eye travels not across but up and down,
Where the oldest inhabitant is a ruffled sheep
Chewing in the rain or stubborn by a gate,
Dogs to be called in several languages
And the sun lighting up the windows of our neighbours.

Our glasses are empty. The windows growing dark.
There are things that I want to tell you, but the occasion
Forbids it. And if there is anything for you to say,
That chance has already gone. What we take
From encounters like this is finally only the sense
Of how we must salvage everything that we can
From the tide that casts us up on the shore of our lives
At every moment, wave upon wave upon wave.

For you that future has been unexpectedly cancelled
And I must take care to remember your best advice
About history, for in the one chance we have
Between 'Take care, laddie' and 'Watch out, matey'
Lies the always threatening gap of the crucial decision
That is either a one-way bridge or a shared relief.
If there is anyone now whose words we are glad
To listen to, we shall be lucky, uncle.

Europe

1

That swirling from Archangel to Gibraltar
Signals the sort of weather we are under.
We know that maps, like institutions, alter
And sticky days give way to evening thunder.
The globe turns round and countries shift their borders,
And satellites observe the tanks and clouds.
Only the rain will not respond to orders.
Only the sky will not break up like crowds.

The wonder is that Europe can survive:
Like a great dinner-service, chipped and cracked,
Reconstituted, lost, its use unlearned,
While all the guests are flushed by half-past five,
Mindful of precedence but not of tact.
The talk too loud. The odd chair overturned.

2

The plains swept them in from Asia like a wind.
It was the hope of water, where their star
Sank to refresh itself. But they had sinned,
And their forgiveness always seemed too far.
The mountains held them in suspense like breath,
Thick forests haunted every settlement,
Night told them stories of a living death
And exile nursed them everywhere they went.

And they were Europe's first romantics. Rome
Had bequeathed a stoic temper, and the cross
Made pleasure something it was worth forgetting.
The sadness of the Slav was different: home
Neither law nor heaven but a state of loss,
Songs full of sobs, the sun forever setting.

3

Borders that roads made into mountain passes,
Cultures that visitors admired and bought,
Languages acquired in language classes,
Religions carefully preserved and taught,
Quarrels converted into fear by taxes
And wars that art made into monuments
Became the rim of a great wheel whose axis
Turned on no more than mythical events:

The sky that speaks, a hero who can fly,
The founding father suckled by a bear,
The wandering race that finds a home at last,
And other lies: the lie of destiny,
The lie of law, and then the lie we care
About the most, that lies lie in the past.

4

Consider the slow gains of the settled life,
The bargains and the prizes of the soil,
Herds of the mother yielded with a wife,
Walls of the son rewarded for his toil
And questions they decided once by fighting
Across a stream that only said 'Perhaps'
Turned in the sharper certainties of writing
To powerful dogma in their deeds and maps.

But there's no argument that will not suffer
From being the point at which the bloodshed starts.
Law is the prior possession of the land
When hate was understood and justice rougher,
And law will sink its claws into our hearts
Till there is nothing left to understand.

5

At their first sight of it they came to know
Pure terror and for once were quite alone.
Earth had no larger absences to show.
This restless emptiness was like their own.
Their souls were mirrored in its treeless spaces.
Its livelihood became a game to learn.
The ownership of routes instead of places,
Horizons that you head towards not yearn.

So, following the darting towns of fishes,
They named each current as they named a peak,
Observed the tides and were surprised no more
To know the stars and compass of their wishes.
This was the blessing they had come to seek,
And paused in prayer when they stepped ashore.

6

We have this image in our politics
Of calm republics of the self, sand-hot
Oases of dreaming, where the mind can fix
Upon its fruitful hatreds, writing what
The Crusoe of our conscience calls its legal
But guilty hoarding of a dwindled stock,
Alphonse with his lighthouse and his eagle,
Or Pincher Martin on his saving rock.

Islands of preaching cormorants or nudes
Are all our castles now. What the king said
Ordered the verbs to venerate his noun,
That most unwelcome of all solitudes,
Exploited islands, islands of the dead,
The dirty rascals always getting down.

7

Islands have better secrets than you think.
The gnarled and rearing shoreline drives you back
A bobbing distance on the cream and ink
To sink a hopeful anchor. Or the track
That winds inland turns on itself again
And simply brings you to a different bay.
The mountains disappear. It starts to rain,
The march put off until another day.

But at the heart the fires still smoulder on,
The passes blackened that you need to cross,
The wooded valleys glowing in their embers.
And if there once were roads, the roads have gone,
And stones in villages record no loss
That anyone has witnessed or remembers.

8

The Turk at length withdrew like a tired lover
And all Vienna breathed into a waltz,
Informers blown to pieces with their cover
And emperors forgiven with their faults,
Religions left on rocks like prison islands
And borders argued over like old toys,
Resentment manoeuvring in utter silence
And townships breaking up in dirt and noise.

It seems the sentries never left their posts,
Their weapons barely sheathed. The information
Whispered in hatred by their tribal ghosts
Contained a single word: a lie, a nation.
Now it is Europe's stinking armpit and
Unravelling sleeve. And clenched, uplifted hand.

9

That's him. There. Arrogantly in our sights,
Strolling upon the ridge. It's easy to
Adjust the barrel's angle as he lights
A cigarette, and shakes the match. For who
Believes a war is started by one bullet?
Or that the slight resistance of the trigger
Could urge the curling forefinger to pull it?
Who would believe his enemy a figure
Whose very insignificance would then
Become a symbol of a natural process
By which the logic breeds that in all men
Has been a prior condition of psychosis? –
Steeling the will until the heart is stilled
And knowing only this: kill, or be killed.

10

The age of empires is forever passing.
The ancient centre of administration
And all the roads that led there slowly grassing
Over, every province now a nation
Blooming uniquely like a grafted flower,
Enthralling as a hostess who dismisses
Her soirée at an unexpected hour,
False as the seal of diplomatic kisses.

Nations in turn exist uncertainly.
Their delegates, like guests, arrive too late
In shabby suits for all-important sessions
Where simply how it's spelled will guarantee
That torture takes the name of a new state,
And maps are issued in minute impressions.

11

Suppose I cut your head off with a saw?
People wake up remembering what I did
With eyelids, folded stumps of ears still raw,
The filthy nose swung open like a lid.
How did those features ever once compose
A face? And gaze in fear or in reproach
At blood still welling deeply like a rose
Or crusting on the shoulders like a brooch?

Before she died, a shadow in her eyes
Entered my eyes, lodged in their caves of bone.
The head became a thing of curious size
And tumbled damply to the meadow, as
A foal drops from its mother. Like my own,
That head contained what guilt the body has.

12

And then the creatures spoke. To some the question
Of whether the bear was sleeping or awake
Simply depended on the bear's digestion,
No likelihood of slumber being fake.
Others voiced miscellaneous objections:
They were not jackals. Despite their best endeavour
The union was bound to cause defections.
A Balkan winter would not last for ever.

Remember what the actual jackals said:
'The interest of jackals everywhere
Lies in the pack. The jackal who doesn't run
With us betrays us, might as well be dead.'
And what the bear observed: 'To be a bear
Takes not the slightest effort. I am one.'

13

Not an unbroken landscape where a dreamer
Might wander with an idea for a day,
Coming unharmed at last to what will seem a
Friendly village, having lost his way;
Not an undifferentiated language which
Strange men on lonely roads could use when meeting
And neither of them ends up in a ditch,
Having conveyed a threat, intending greeting.

For lines of speech are like horizons where
Something lies hidden that might blow apart
The frank, the open-armed, the undecided,
And dialects and borders will not spare
The best intentions of the mind or heart
To act as though they'd never been divided.

14

Within the architecture of effect
Fear has compiled its special regulations:
A system of repression to protect,
Façades as grimly closed as occupations.
Outside the towns the track runs as it must
Between the innocent and wooded hills.
Fields stretch for miles and crops grow in the dust
Where man and weather work their separate wills.

A state reveals its nature at its border.
A nervous guard, his eyes like thumb-tacks, glancing
Briefly at passports, moving correctly down
The train, everything more or less in order.
Just yards ahead, in Greece, singing and dancing.
Behind, for every pair of boots, a frown.

15

So little difference. A length of bread
Or wire can separate the living wraith
From the no-longer miserable dead.
A length of lip, an accent or a faith
Is like a signature upon a warrant,
The certain failure of some nightmare test
That proves your very choice of life abhorrent
To those who wish to see you dispossessed.

The sunny street you learned to cycle down
Is closed this year. The girls have gone away.
The purses of your fig-tree will not split
Their gold with you. The buses heading into town
Won't stop. And all the time, day after day,
It was to be. Though no one mentioned it.

16

That shape beneath your arm. Is it a gun?
What are your fingers turning over there?
What is that object glinting in the sun?
Dodging for cover, there's no time to stare,
Only to fire. As you would fire on me,
Unable to let that crucial moment pass,
If only to restore the strange normality
Of running doubled over dogs and glass
To reach the safety of an alley's shade.
And there are many more where you have been
And some are still alive and some are dead.
I cannot see the loaves and coins, afraid
Of what I know: the difference between
A line of snipers and a queue for bread.

17

In many ways a meaningless event:
A slight misjudgement, the last hurdle dented,
An unexpected Greek by accident
Winning in games her country once invented.
But who could not detect in her elation
A pride that utterly transformed her face,
Made her both individual and nation,
The dual champion of her lucky race?

Precisely these emotions and this cheering
Deafens elsewhere the hated and the humbled,
For pride itself is double, and is reckoned
Upon the finest calculations, fearing
All common excellence. The girl who stumbled
Condemned to weeping shame by half a second.

18

The map is like a cloudscape lit by flares,
And Serbia, Kosovo, Albania, Greece is
Like a chess position where the squares
Are haunted by the shadows of the pieces,
Where every possibility contains
Too many other possibilities
For any certain outcome, and the brain's
Exhausted by the lines it thinks it sees.

And policy is only what will prove
That there were very few alternatives.
Or that, though different, they were much the same.
The move you end up making is the move
That you were always going to make. Which gives
Excuses to the losers in the game.

19

To be the powers! To sit with microphones
At tables gently circular as the
Great globe itself, speaking aloud from thrones
Disguised as sofas, turning photography
Into an hourly ikon of their trust,
Their rage and their responsibility!
The powers are never threatened. If they must,
They will react to power. And agree.

But hearts are fragile to enforce a bond.
Not a blade's fineness but its fore-edge weight
Counts most, they say, in the cutting of the knife.
Only at length, and wearily, they respond
To the pert brandished arguments of state,
Never to something broken like a life.

20

A resolution will not force compassion.
Pain makes no contribution to ballistics.
No interested government can fashion
Occasions of weeping out of cold statistics.
And though the silent headlines keep accounts
Of all these dispossessions to be faced,
Two million, three, impossible amounts,
Europe again impossibly disgraced,
There's nothing after all we can afford
More easily than easy opinion,
That there is only sympathy to give
The homeless, when the least to be restored
Is somewhere to return to when all's done,
Not very different from a place to live.

21

'Yes, they are saved, and all they have endured
Forgotten. The smallest, dangled on my arm,
Reaches the flight of mercy, will be cured
Of life. These others death will never harm.
They will be children always.' Still we ask
Why have they stopped saving the children now?
Hasn't it only just begun, this task,
Now that we know it must be done, but how?

The sky is silent, and a wind blows through
The smashed windows of buses. Somewhere a child
Crouches behind a gun, his finger curled
Upon the trigger. Children soon learn to do
What must be done, their bodies raked and piled.
If we could save them we could save the world.

22

Stretched in its coastal slumber in the sun
The full length of the continental shelf,
Paws round the captured Mediterranean,
Europe continues to admire itself.
The painful tongue of an immense devouring
Opens the foetid wounds of its old age.
The smell of wickedness is overpowering.
We hear the slamming of its summer cage.

We are its willing keepers. Every day
We speak the soothing words it likes to hear:
Whoever is dead will stay for ever dead,
Whatever happens, happens anyway,
Whatever we do, we do it out of fear,
Whatever is said, there's nothing to be said.

Corsica, August 1992

61

Quartet

The Duke String Quartet in Trinity College Chapel

The sound's diagonal, like oars. Its space is
Also made of wood: the altar's square
Geometry of light, the framing faces
Of carved startled children, pair by pair;
The strut of column, urn and cornice topped
By an ascent of drapery and toes.
The pulsing heartache of the strings is stopped
By pressure of the fingers and the bows.

It must be the medium's nature to be profuse:
Grain of rose in its rubbed lake of wood
Offers a panelled ear (or is it an eye?)
To reflect the voyaging mind. Along the pews
Heads are inclined like saints' who know they could
Endure this exultation till they die.

Metropolitan

In cities there are tangerine briefcases on the down-platform
and jet parkas on the up-platform; in the mother of cities
there is equal anxiety at all terminals.
*West a business breast, North a morose jig, East a false
escape, South steam in milk.*

The centres of cities move westwards; the centre of the
mother of cities has disappeared.
*North the great cat, East the great water, South the great
fire, West the great arrow.*

In cities the sons of women become fathers; in the mother
of cities the daughters of men have failed to become mothers.
*East the uneager fingers, South the damp cave, West the
chained ankle, North the rehearsed cry.*

Cities are built for trade, where women and men may freely
through knowing each other become more like themselves;
the mother of cities is built for government, where women
and men through fearing each other become more like each
other than they care to be.
*South the short, West the soap, North the sheets, East the
shivers.*

In cities the church fund is forever stuck below blood heat;
in the mother of cities the church is a community arts centre.
*West the Why-not, North the Now-then, East the End-product,
South the Same-again.*

In cities nobody can afford the price; in the mother of cities
nobody dares to ask the price.
*North the telephone smile, East the early appointment,
South the second reminder, West the hanging button.*

In cities the jealous man is jealous because he is himself in his imagination unfaithful; in the mother of cities the jealous man is jealous because he reads the magazines.

East the endless arrival, South the astounding statistic, West the wasted words, North the night of nights.

In cities we dream about our desire; in the mother of cities we dream about our dreams.

Pheasant and Mulberry

As to put up with damp in a cave and
Its unremovable jewels is to
Claim the weird cogitation of grottoes

Or against beechmast to take a flying kick
Then stoop to nibble in acquisitive
Content is to comprehend granaries

So within the wild garden of the mind
Reality surely excels itself:
Two pheasants paired beneath a mulberry,

Economical sketch by the sexual
Philosopher, there pacing out a loss,
Or worse, the absence of the never-claimed.

Much meditation may see a design
In the fall of fruit, the pheasants' slow dance,
An imagined labyrinth dictating

Satisfied puzzles, willed speculation,
Maps in flagstones, directions in hedges,
Everything that defines a centre.

Most of us have known these languid moods
When we create and discreate ourselves
In the landscape of our fugitive thoughts.

Grotto, granary, garden, labyrinth
Are pleased to design the impossible
As our sadness at envisaging it

So that every little tread in the grass,
Each stain or husk, is an almost noiseless
Echo of the world we have to live in.

Logical Exercises

A1.   The tree enters the body in the form of a god.
  2.   Matter is everything that doesn't matter.
  3.   Manna is a divine rebuke.
  4.   Simultaneous was the discovery of crops and of the transmigration of souls.
  5.   The flower longs to be fruit.
  6.   The birth of the lamb is also a miracle.
  7.   The righteous are those who can control their dreams.
  8.   Nomads learn to expect hunger.
  9.   Stories are the food of the soul.
10.   The tree leaves the body in the form of the planet.

B1.   Freedom is an illusion of the organism.
  2.   Grandmothers hunger for what they already know.
  3.   The greatest freedom would be to live for ever.
  4.   Wicked is the god who decreed hunger.
  5.   Nothing is adored by mistake.
  6.   The motion of the wolf is the desire for independence.
  7.   The fat boy is hungry for stories about woodcutters.
  8.   Longing joins the active molars with the planet.
  9.   No nomad is a woodcutter.
10.   There is no such thing as the solitary life.

C1.   Fruit inches through the body.
  2.   The worm aches to displace the soil.
  3.   The teeth meet in the bone-marrow.
  4.   The woodcutter never goes hungry.
  5.   Gods have no need for stories.
  6.   The thrush mistakes the udder.
  7.   Desert food arrives from nowhere.
  8.   Yeasts adore the tree.
  9.   The wasp craves for pig cheese.
10.   Illusory also is the stitched belly full of stones.

D1. Fruit dies into our dreams.
 2. Nothing can imagine a life that is not already its own.
 3. The dreams of nomadic tribes struggle for
                                        permanence.
 4. No man is lonely when he eats.
 5. Digestion is the defiance of species.
 6. No god rebukes a righteous man.
 7. The flower squirms on its root like the fat boy
                              wanting to be excused.
 8. No god is an animal.
 9. The soul leaves the body in sleep and drunkenness.
10. There are many stories about trees and wolves and
                                              gods.

E1. A god would rather be adored than eaten.
 2. The grandmother's words are forgotten.
 3. Illusions are sinful unless agreed to be illusions.
 4. We long for what we know we have no means of
                                        imagining.
 5. Men would like to be gods.
 6. Loneliness is nothing but the imagining of other lives.
 7. The woodcutter's wife suckles the lamb.
 8. Killing to eat is an assertion of rootlessness.
 9. God reminds us of our sins by turning himself into a
                                              tree.
10. Writing was invented to record material things.

Barbed Wire Blues

Hear that wild dog hollering?
Keep him out with Two-Staple Wing,
Roll me some Two-Staple Wing, yes, and make it plenty,
My baby has ten fingers and a throat to croon and sing.

No ways he going to reach you, girl.
Keep him out with Merrill Twirl,
Roll me Merrill Twirl, yes, and keep it rolling,
My baby has a mile of hair and starlight every curl.

Roll me Brink Flat, roll me Buckthorn,
Roll me Baker Perfect.
Never know what I'm expecting,
Post and wire is for protecting,
Still more fences to be pegged.

Pray that if he leaps he miss.
Keep him out with Oval Twist,
Roll me Oval Twist, yes, and make it bristle,
My baby has a tongue moves like a contortionist.

What makes him think he's getting down?
Keep him out with Wrap-Round,
Roll me Wrap-Round, yes, and make it double,
My baby has a couple of legs reach right to the ground.

Roll me Old Square, roll me Half Round,
Roll me Haish and Glidden.
Tug it, turn the loop and bend up,
Where I start is where I end up,
Ripped-up hands is all I get.

Tell that dog to take a trip.
Keep him out with Scutts Clip,
Roll me some Scutts Clip, yes, and pack it thick,
My baby has a low-slung rear cracks like a rawhide whip.

How's that wild thing getting in?
Keep him out with 4 Point 1 Between,
Roll me 4 Point 1 Between, yes, and nail it clean,
My baby has the tightest little snatch you ever seen.

Roll me Stubbs Plate, roll me Sawtooth,
Roll me Kelly's Knife Blade.
Plugging staples, three days riding,
Skin was never made for hiding,
Still they find her where she lies,
Still they find her where she lies.

A Cuclshoc

Not the new racquets themselves, strung
To the pitch of drums in that wiry meshed black
Of loudspeakers. Not the crammed tube of feathers.

They are a daughterly indulgence, gear
To stir the sluggish pumps and muscles of our fifties,
Mythical as the breath they need, and tan knees.

Not these, which seem a flattering novelty,
But a letter found later in a dusty trunk
Brings to mind all that I know of this game.

Brings it back across a half century
In a cautious upper case and licked pencil
That once imagined Blackpool for Nairobi.

The signifiers are elementary. I HAVE
GOT A CUCLSHOC. I CAN HIT IT
5 TIMS. What else do I remember?

The cistern drip and chill of an attic Christmas.
The layered curves of the frames, stained maroon
Like spills, and trussed with yellow woven gut.

And the rattling thwung of the wobbly cork tub
Bound with its brittle stumps of varnished feathers
That however hard you hit it, slowed, and turned.

It made me think of the parson's nose, all quills:
When it wavered towards me over the washing-line
It was like getting ready to biff a chicken's bum.

And if I missed, although it had stopped dead
Mysteriously in mid-air, it dropped just too quickly
Out of my reach, like a newsreel commando.

Whatever I might have known about adult love,
About the sacred triviality of letters
Or their conspiracy at a distance about presents,

Whatever I suspected might be uncertain in the future,
In the size of oceans, the licensed irregularity
Of wars and the accuracy of torpedoes,

Cries out from these laborious sentences
With all their childish feeling and now with all
My later tears. I HOPE YOU WILL COM BACK SOON

SO WE CAN HAVE SOM FUN. That winged basket,
That little lofted button, forever hovering,
Still hangs in the back yard, beyond my racquet.

The feathers are splayed in the sun, like the fragile words
We sometimes write and mean, which therefore always
Mean and always will be there to do so.

SEND A FOTORGAF OF YOR SELF. It glints
With the stitching of angels, buoyant in the light,
Never falling. WELL WELL GOOD BY DADDY DEAR.

Heartmelt

The treacherous blue of the hollow snow
And the ancient blue of the gletscher
Are like the flicker of a headache
Or the acid of the etcher
Making transparent what was opaque,
And now the haunting, oh so slow
Beginning of movement, the light of ice
Dripped from a lip of rock, showing
The sun what beacons are, the glint
And dribble of the water flowing
Freely now, falling without stint,
Once each drop has fallen twice:
The danger is past, as we have long felt:
Though mountains are still there, the mountains melt.

Sunflowers

The surging of a star
Makes moons of umber
Many-million-grained,
Bowed like dejected dolls
In ragged slumber.

Penitent in their pews,
Their only reason
To turn and turn about,
Tilting up their bonnets
For a short season.

Hope for them was a halo
Of chrome petals
Worn with utter devotion
Till the gaze became a mask
Of the deepest of metals.

Impossible to conceive
Of such a hero
Whose indiscriminate eye
Passed over them unseeing,
A moral zero.

Passed, and is passing now
Over the errors
That we have often sown,
Over the stumps of crops
And other terrors.

For hatred in the earth
In neighbour and nation
Grows equally and tall
Though it hang its head
In exculpation.

Though it wept in the dust,
Though it pleaded
For one more second of life,
The fruit has broken open
And the fruit is seeded.

Saint August in his robes,
Praising his maker,
Treads in the burning fields
A passage through each ranked
And guilty acre.

Edward Lear in Corsica

*Is it not unpleasant, at fifty-six years of age, to feel that it
is increasingly probable that a man can never hope to be
otherwise than alone, never, no, never more? Did not Edgar
Poe's raven distinctly say 'Nevermore'?*
     Edward Lear, *Journal of a Landscape Painter*

With its colourful flora and fauna
How delightful to visit La Corse!
There is silence for once in the corner:
Poe's raven has cried himself hoarse.

The terrible word that he utters
Brings none of its usual fears.
In Ajaccio, latched are the shutters
And deep are the hats over ears.

For hope is a buoyant statistic
And here they are used to being free.
You are bound to become optimistic
When you wander into the maquis.

The woods breathe a whimsical vapour
That doesn't compel you to think.
The walks by the shore smell like paper.
The sea is the colour of ink.

The landscape was formed when the planet
Had little but rocks on its mind.
The fall of the coastline granite
Is awesome but not unkind.

When the clock chimes five and a quarter
Already I've fought with the sea.
I rise from the vanquished water
And drip from my beard to my knee.

My pride, like a low-tide anemone
Is sailing at less than full rig
And my otherwise pendulous gemini
Are tight as a Cargèse fig.

I shall live in crepuscular mountains
Where the chestnuts are full of white cows.
I shall drink at the pebbly fountains
And put on a peasant's loose blouse.

I shall draw every day what's before me.
My spirit will put up a fight.
Not a thing on this island could bore me.
I shall map the behaviour of light.

Here's the pichet. Now take out the stopper.
Through my breakfast I'll know who I am.
The honey's the colour of copper.
The wine is the colour of jam.

The fish are the colour of roses.
The cheese is the colour of cheese.
Its smell has found out where the nose is.
The name of it sounds like a sneeze.

In heaven one stores up treasure
From every shifting mood
That belongs to the landscape of pleasure
With its rituals of air and of food.

The host of the morning croissant,
The sacrament of the pêche,
The globulous soupe des poissons
That is almost an act of the flesh.

The tone of a leaf or a petal,
The wind with its breath of intrigue,
The herbs that seduce from the kettle,
The herbs that define the garrigue.

But it's on to the col de Bavella!
Where the mountains are pink in the sky
Like the ribs of a lady's umbrella
Left out in the garden to dry.

The easel unfolds like a table.
There is oil, and fresh pigments to crush.
With a sweep of my hand I am able
To lay on the sky with a brush.

In each cloud, in each pine, in each boulder
You may see that the paint hasn't lied.
Come sir, look over my shoulder:
The hills are like elephant's hide.

There was a young lady of Zonza –
But I cannot come up with a rhyme.
My verse-making skill has quite gone, sir.
I find that I haven't the time.

It was something to do with a corset,
Or was it the shape of her toes?
When the memory's gone you can't force it.
God knows where the memory goes.

The past is a prison. I've tried it.
It is choked up with ash like a grate.
The future has nothing inside it.
The present is hard to locate.

I have made an important decision:
I shall live from now on in my art.
It's a way to achieve the precision
That's dulled in affairs of the heart.

The nourishing zest of the highlight
That glints from a rock or a spoon,
The deepening draught of the twilight,
The rich chiaroscuro of noon.

And then, when the starlight is silent
Above the still murmurous sea,
I shall know I belong to this island
And this island belongs to me.

And I shall have found the haven,
That glistening granular shore,
Where flown is the ruminous raven
And the echo is: 'Evermore!'

'Prudence dans l'Eau'

Far from being a warning,
Today's newspaper horoscope
Is simply a tender description
Of this aquarelle you enact
As if by a maître of 1919

For whom the maillot, beyond
Its masquerading as a garment,
Becomes the tracing of a line
Negotiating a containment
Of convalescent blue.

You may picture the sea
As a requirement of masses:
Here, the caution of shoulders
A shade of biscuit against
A disintegrating wall of wave.

There, the wide wash of azure
With its pucker of cobalt
And unsettling flung creams.
And further, just off-centre,
The teacherly red tick of a sail.

It's not that you're happy to become this picture.
You're happy for once to be yourself,
Cradled in water that moves forever
Over the stones and fishes of the morning,
Beneath the stones and fires of night.

Canicule Macaronique

Heureux ceux qui ont la clim
          Corse-Matin (6:8:94)

Heureux ceux qui ont la clim
Pendant la grande canicule.
Heureux those whose culs are cool.
Heureuse her and heureux him.

C'est la canicule qui hurle,
Ready to tear you limb from limb.
Heureux ceux qui ont la clim,
Cri-criant: 'O turlútuturle!'

La situation est grim,
The mise-en-scène a trifle burle.
À chaleur disons donc: 'Ta gueule!'
And keep ourselves amused and slim.

Heureux qui par terre se roule:
Lucky Luke and Lucky Jim,
Edith Piaf, Tiger Tim,
Et le plus divin Poupoule.

Heureux Toccate, heureux Hymne,
Heureux Mouvements Perpetuels,
Heureuses Les Bîches immortelles,
De tristesse sexuelle synonyme.

Je ne regrette rien. I'm full
Of love as are the seraphim,
And plein de bonheur to the brim,
Pendant cette grande canicule.

La vie has satisfying sym:
For every lui there lives an elle.
Finding its level in her well,
La source sauvage is in the swim.

Ni ouragan ni canicule,
Ni pretexte prompte ou assez flim,
Can keep le coeur from feeling imm,
Allègre in the planet's pull.

Let's fly together in a bim,
Au-dessus de la fou-foule
Qui mange ses menus et ses moules,
Impregné de sueur, et prim!

For always I'll have you, and you'll
Have me, and though desire grows dim,
Heureux ceux qui ont la quim,
Heureuses celles qui ont le tool.

Forever through the sky will skim
Le pé-pédalo de Dédale,
Escaladant sans escale
The blue horizon's endless rim.

En pénitence, le tournesol
Beguiné, poudreux, anonyme,
Turns and turns, and at a whim
Sonne, en sol, son son du sol.

From Chatellerault to Arles and Nîmes
Le visage bronze du tournesol
S'incline comme un pa-parasol
Trouve une épaule coquette, intime.

Devisé dans le banderole:
'Heureux ceux qui ont la clim.'
Across the fields the notes are dim:
Son sol, son sol, son sol, son sol.

Star-Gazing

1

This glass is open to the sky
And gives the spaces overhead
(Which only never seem to die
Because they are already dead)
Their bright particularity.

They terrify us with their roar
Of silence and their sprawling lack
Of definition. They ignore
The names we give them as they pour
Their startling shapes against the black.

And in its quivering circle they
Return our gaze with unconcern
As though they only had to burn
And burn, and might not even stay
Till all their light had burned away.

It is a stiff and heavy glass,
Turning within a thread of brass.
It is an eye to frame at night
The airy meteors as they pass
And read their signatures of light.

It has no legs on which to stand
But must be shouldered and then panned,
The eyepiece steadied with one hand,
The other acting as support
Until the looked-for star is caught.

And this is how, in any case,
We tend to use the tilted face:
The naked eye a searching cone,
The straining neck leant back, alone
Or on a shoulder not its own.

Star-gazing is a friendly thing,
When eyes aware of other eyes
And other arms on which to cling
Seek fires of a different size
And arcs that colder clay supplies.

And that discrepancy of sense
Restores us to each other, hence
To our exalted littleness
From which we dare thus to address
The neighbourhood of the immense.

Remember when the season bid
Us wander up and down the hill,
Blinking against the sky until
Its blackness bore a Perseid,
A little spark that seemed to spill?

The dizzy heavens tried to weep
With stars, the night was nearly gold,
We clenched our fingers counting, told
Tall stories till at last the cold
Conveyed us to the house of sleep.

2

The telescope's one dusty eye
Was found beneath my father's bed,
Coffined and latched. I don't know why
He kept it there. He might instead
Have let me point it at the sky.

We could have looked for every star
Named on his little planisphere,
Making the scattered singular
And with a word bring strangely near
The very farthest of the far.

For language is this human trick
Of simply daring to presume
Upon the contents of a room,
Distinguishing, quadruple quick,
A chess queen from a candlestick.

Since we have words for the unseen
And places where we've never been,
It's not surprising we know how
We can discriminate between
Cassiopeia and the Plough.

The I and Not-I is another,
Learnt by the baby from its mother
When first it predicates the Other,
But this is going too far back
Into the Freudian zodiac.

And anyway you will recall
How Freud declared that after all
Our devious minds turn everything
To something else: imagining
A breast, we dream a piece of Ming.

Are things the same, or different?
We take our pleasure in the trope
Of metaphor, where what is meant
Is not what's said: a star is hope,
And longing is a telescope.

That sort of thing. Or maybe it's
A poem made of separate bits,
Joining the lid and narrow box
By means of hinges and of locks,
Inevitable opposites.

Or it's the closing of the light,
A deathbed of its own, the pen's
Last stroke, the useless oxygen's
Retreat, the stopped watch in the night
Sharing the darkness of its lens.

Or it's a symbol, if you'd rather,
Of the essentially unknown,
The door that opens with a groan
To leave me standing there alone
In terror, and without a father.

3

Most of us eventually
Are orphans. Now that I am one
At fifty-six, it's real to me
But is a state with which no one
Could really have much sympathy.

For when our story's almost done
The plot is clear, it never thickens:
No deeds turn up, no bastard son,
No cruel change of fortune, none,
Nor tight-lipped guardians out of Dickens.

No shocking secret brings relief,
No birthmarks, sapphires or debentures,
No equatorial adventures,
No cousin with a handkerchief
Or pretty lips to blot the grief.

The twin events were feared and fated
And they were not long separated:
After the closing of his door,
Although my mother watched and waited,
Life could not go on as before.

And so she suddenly departed
And finished what her parents started.
Her final face was broken-hearted:
That mask we never rearrange,
The one expression we can't change.

Less of surprise than resignation,
The mouth almost in supplication.
I looked in vain at that inert
Abstraction, trying to convert
It to rebuke, or love, or hurt.

And his: likewise a spurious cast
Of some imposed solemnity,
A hollow mockery, the last
Gaunt face he pulled to frighten me,
One I could never bear to see.

For all the warnings and the fuss
Death is an instantaneous
Incompetent photographer,
The moment always wrong, a blur
We never could admit was us.

We'd always go back if we could
To that authentic unrehearsed
Expression that we had at first.
We may have thought it not much good
But hadn't then foreseen the worst.

And so my orphaned task is to
Redeem that album of the living
In memory without misgiving.
The lens of death is unforgiving.
The shutter falls for me and you.

4

Perhaps the entire universe
Is something like a camera
Within which matter can rehearse
Its unconvincing poses, star
By star, self-satisfied, perverse.

An endless film is moving through
Its darkness, a grey pantomime,
A shadow of some ballyhoo
That we are bound to misconstrue:
The film is us, is mind, is time.

How can we see and understand?
How can we see and be inside it?
We haven't yet identified it.
We think it is immensely grand
Yet need to hold it in our hand.

That particle that we observe
Appears to take a likely curve
And yet we doubt its path and distance:
Is it the same, or did it swerve?
Has it position *and* existence?

We slave to see electrons glide.
We like to watch the cells divide.
We'd put the sun beneath a slide,
Even our own observing eye,
To try to see our ignorance die.

Forgetting that we found the comic
Ages before the subatomic,
Forgetting the philosophic glories
Of the wise Greeks, observatories
Showing them systems that were stories.

No theories do it half so well
As what the lifted eye can trust:
The sky itself that longs to tell
The fable of its mortal dust
That falls and burns because it must.

Now Sol inflates his fiery chest
And drives his chariot to the west.
Beneath the burning wheels and hooves
The glittering sea grows large. It moves
More slowly now, and takes its rest.

Night loses all her inhibitions
Upon the sleeping of the sun.
The dome is opened, one by one
The stealthy stars take their positions
And act as they have always done.

Their dances formally presage
The entry of the real star,
Nude Artemis, the singular
Pale presence in this theatre,
Striding across her silver stage.

5

In every sky she knows her place.
In Corsica she looks just as
She does in Wales. (In Wales the face
She sadly leans towards us has
The old Oxonian grimace).

Perhaps it's something she forgot?
Her one good eye is vacant, more
Like a bruise, a cobweb or a blot.
And we stare back. But don't know what
On earth she can be looking for.

Something immeasurably lost,
Like innocence? Or something hunted?
Does she look savage, or affronted?
She chose a vagrant's path. The cost:
Millennia of dust and frost.

The tides are at her heels, and she
Reflects a special gravity
On water. Easy then to claim
She has a longing for the sea
From which initially she came.

Here on this plio-quaternian coast
The wind has hollowed each exposed
Piled boulder to a standing ghost,
A gargoyle or a weathered shell,
A sort of lunar sentinel.

So the *tafonu* haunts the rocks,
Bathed in the very light it mocks,
A gaunt subspheric demilune,
A meteorological cartoon,
A granite version of the moon.

It takes no time for the grotesque
To normalise its strange aesthetic:
It constitutes the picturesque,
Its likenesses are energetic
And are essentially poetic.

How readily they can disarm,
These sculptures of the Notre Dame
De la Serra or Calanches de Piana!
Configurations of Diana,
Wrecked symbols of her power to charm.

They are the metaphors of change;
Of matter's endless vacillation
And dogged differentiation,

Its power to seem forever strange:
Analogies of alienation.

So we stare down the littoral,
Just as we calculate the night,
For stalactite or meteorite,
Behaviour of stone or light
Departing from the usual.

6

For we have stripped away the year
With grief and work, and found its heart,
Something with which to persevere,
Something with which to make a start,
Something we knew we might find here.

The summer shows us at its core
A state of being that might save us.
What we have lost we can't restore,
But know we have, and need therefore,
The bodies that our mothers gave us.

Our eyes, grown heavier with all
They've seen, need lifting up towards
The light. We need those major chords,
That full acceptance of the sprawl
Of nature in her free-for-all.

We need the sea's oblivion,
To dive below and gaze upon
The coloured life that knows no clocks,
The *oblade* and the *sparaillon*
Playful beneath their crusted rocks.

And where the water meets the sun,
Burnished when the day is done,
The sea and sky appear as one,

Rare stuffs laid out that no bazaar
Could sell: faded, crepuscular.

The late sky's only silhouette
Are hills that few have crossed as yet
Or wish to cross, for on each side
Are valleys where men lived and died
And never were unsatisfied.

The tumbling bat comes out to eat
And crickets open their salon.
The lizard poses at your feet,
Then moves with practised flourish on
The dust it owns and signs, Anon.

Again we light the candles and
Make shadows of our contraband
Of herb and shell, and once again
We pour the pink wine of Sartène
And hold its pebbles in our hand.

At which we come to feel, of course,
With vacillating Arnold, 'Ah
Love, let us, etcetera . . .'
But feel it with unusual force
Beneath the heavens' *feux de joie*.

And wish for it beneath their beams
And watch the orange lily burn
To black against the sky and learn
Again the names of stars and turn
From the flickering terrace to our dreams.

7

Our dreams are how the past arrives
At compromise. They come in clusters,
Like jostling men concealing knives;

Or singly, the strict loss-adjusters
Of over-accidental lives.

Just as distressingly, they go.
Whether unique or in a series
They do not, like a video,
Record the things we ought to know
Or illustrate important theories.

They are not baleful like a spook
Or tie things neatly like a suture,
They do not speak about the future
In riddles like the Pentateuch,
Issue no warning or rebuke.

Yet sometimes out of our obsessions,
Our cautiousness, our indiscretions,
Our dreaming minds intently make
Surprising symbols of repressions
They can do nothing with awake.

Here we sleep long, remember more,
And our unconscious when we snore
Stands open like a friendly door
Revealing our individual isness
Struggling to sublimate life's business.

The frequent dream we never doubt
Or think to ask what it's about
Takes on new certainty, its theme
Acknowledged in the general scheme
Of what we recognise as dream.

That hidden staircase, undetected,
Leads to a half-remembered room.
The smouldering timbers, long neglected,
May breathe each cinder to a plume,
And break into a fiery bloom.

And yet I climb excited there
To find some sort of foothold where
I might do something to reclaim it.
I know I do not need to name it:
The stair's the thrill of being a stair.

And it is almost less surprising
Than the reality around us.
When in the morning fish surround us,
This is because we swim on rising,
Yet still our equilibrium founders:

Half-asleep we glide, mistaking
The weedy rocks for grassy vales,
See distant sheep instead of snails
And crows for the black scissory tails
Of *castagnoles* we know on waking.

8

And if we wake up in the night,
We easily feel flabbergasted:
Our dream had such vast scope, despite
Our knowing that it must have lasted
No longer than a meteorite.

A whole Victorian triple-decker
Is there, the scientists have reckoned,
All the emotion of *Rebecca*,
All the excitement of *The Wrecker*,
Contained within a microsecond.

Our dreams burn up on entering
The atmosphere of real life.
They snap shut like a pocket-knife,
Are delphic, tiny, maddening
As prisoned birds that will not sing.

What was it that my father said
To my cocooned and dreaming head?
He sat there, dazed, and I was not
Surprised to see he was not dead.
I talked on like an idiot:

The multitudinous happenings
Since he had left us, publishings,
Memorials, his personal things,
How I'd looked after their removal,
Hoping I met with his approval.

And yet all this was to protect
Him from the certain ill-effect
Of his decline, the little chance
Of permanent deliverance.
His face took on a radiance.

With all my silly chatter done,
I put my arms about him, knew
His real dying had begun
And knew this miracle was true,
Occasion for a last adieu.

But what he said, or what I made
Him say, was lost. Was I afraid
To hear, or even make the attempt?
Perhaps that moment was undreamt,
A kind of deference to his shade.

And I awoke or I was woken
By a strange consciousness of tons
Of falling stardust fired like guns
Above me, and my dream was broken
By midnight and the weight of suns.

The bright stars flipped like shuttlecocks
That lurch and fall. Each left a mark
Upon the retina, a spark,

A sudden match struck in the dark
That spurts and dies against the box.

9

Alpha Centauri in the night
Look down and tell me what to think.
Pour out unstinting, as I write,
Over my intermittent ink
Your steady undistracted light.

You are the starting point of what
Has been an idle whim of ours:
To draw a line from dot to dot
In the right order, thus to plot
A secret picture of the stars.

Of light you are the principal
Among the many lights that blaze.
You are the entrance to the maze,
The illuminated capital,
The hidden theme of the chorale.

And all we need is your immense
And unconcerned magnificence
Turning and turning unrevealed,
A random point of reference,
One intersection in the field.

I mean, we simply need to start
And all else follows, part by part:
The heavens turn, and through the art
Of imitation we can feel
Them turn, and so invent the wheel.

Then nature's spiral yields the spring,
Whose impetus from tightening
Controls the otherwise hotchpotch

Of random forces. Then a notch
Upon the wheel invents the watch.

Never so simple, but forgive
An argument that goes slipshod!
My real intent is figurative:
In Lilliput it wasn't odd
They thought his watch was Lemuel's god.

For when our hour of death arrives,
We all admit it's time that drives
Us on and that our only heaven
Has been the less than thirty-seven
Million minutes of our lives.

We can't contrive perpetual motion.
Alpha to Omega is more
Than we shall ever have. Three score
And ten concludes our self-devotion,
While the stars dash upon the shore.

Forgive this clockwork replica
Of what we do not understand.
And let our fretful cells disband
In peace beneath each stopped spread hand
And still heart of our Omega.

10

Strange how our jealous star conceals
From us all other stars as though
Their coded clusters, spokes and wheels
Might point us out a way to go!
Empty and blue are his ideals.

And he intends to lull us with
A spurious sense of being free,
Dazzling the senses with his myth

Of a benevolent coppersmith
Burnishing the sky and sea.

But when the sun has gone to rest
The scenic blue gives way to night.
The constellations reignite,
Harmonious, ordered, self-possessed,
The ancient *mécanique céleste*.

Which of their portents can be true?
For me, perhaps, as well as you
There's nothing much they can foretell
That isn't just our point of view:
Stars shine *away* from us as well.

For certain, even while we're gaping,
Their light is rapidly escaping,
So which events they may be shaping
Is much in question: light doesn't last.
The present soon becomes the past.

So all our history is sent
In light-waves through the firmament,
Continuous record of mishaps,
The most extemporised of maps,
The very picture of Perhaps.

And as one scene succeeds the other,
Each generation is distinguished,
Father and son, daughter and mother,
One by one, the bonds relinquished,
And the long lives in turn extinguished.

No pattern there, except in death,
The stubborn drawing of a breath
After breath after breath that perseveres
For all of our allotted years,
The sixtieth, seventieth, eightieth.

So when we look up at the sky
And claim the interest of the stars
And when we weep our au revoirs
We know it is our turn to die.
The next black-letter day is ours.

We even know there's no reprieve
For our own daughters' generation,
Beautiful in their vocation
And individualisation.
And this is what it is to grieve.

from NOW AND FOR A TIME (2002)

Joe's Dream

at the Dartington Summer School of Music

A stillness falls upon him
Though the chords strike up again.
For an hour, the world is dismissed:
Head fallen to one side
And, in repose, a fist.

Sometimes he has been these sounds,
All of them: nothing could hide it.
The lady opened the wonderful box
And he was inside it.
Her fingers touched the strings,
The strings were unsprung locks
And the sound beat up like wings.

Joe, Joe, what do you see?
The mower under the mulberry tree.
The falling mulberry, black as blood,
That leaves the tree for ever,
Alighting with a thud.

Joe, Joe, what do you hear?
Horns of the Hall, 'how thin and clear',
And distant birdsong, like a cry
To hold the summer, trickling off
The edges of the sky.

Behind his fastened eyes
The fairy of the moment
Dances her trick of memory,
An aery nothingness
That promises to stay.

From now on, nothing dies
But enters in that dance:
The bird, the mulberries;

A pair of butterflies
That tumble up the stairs
In air; the garden orchestras.

His head stirs. He sighs.
The world is a great adventure
In which he will take his chance.
Nothing exists till he has tried it.
He wakes, and all the while
The music played, she was the music.
This is her body and her smile,
And he is outside it.

Street Language

1 Pigeons in Balham High Road

This is what you wanted, and what you lean
Out to see from your pushchair: the pigeons
Hunched in the feathered ruffs of their grey greatcoats.

What is it you find to say about these old soldiers?
Is it the startling rise and flutter of broken wings
Above their waddling interest in scraps, the stoical hoarding

And release of rivalrous impulses, that intrigues you?
They are not beautiful, these exiles, but they strike
The attitudes still of their feathered and aerial kind.

Simply they are pavement birds, of the gutter
And fending life. Their memory of exploit
Is like your intuition of its possibility.

For you murmur over their names in your own way,
Your own babble and cooing, that knows what it is
To be so privileged in life as to have such a great idea of it.

2 Fuchsia

What does the flower say, which you have learned to touch
Without tearing, cupping it briefly beneath the chin?
Its bright lips seem to open in wonder, like your own.

You are held up to it, as to the light of a lantern,
And light is all it needs, the adjectival voice of colour,
Repetitive, exclamatory, and at the same time silent.

The garden is red at the ends, as though it had been dipped,
Red and magenta, like the bells of a jester.
It bursts into its still and soundless frenzy.

In this fragrant room without a ceiling, water is trickling
And you are eager again to strangle the green snake.
Yours will be the human language of busy verbs.

The grass is crawling with its own little phrases of wings
    and legs.
The air is full of the flag telegraphy of butterflies.
What does the flower say? Bffzz-tszz-zng-btzzzzz . . .

3 Da

What will the first word be, Daddy or Dog?
Neither are wholly benign, like nursery Nana,
Nor wholly disgraceful, like kennelled Mr Darling.

They are both words you can hammer your tongue under.
Da, you say. Oh! Da, is what it says, too.
Da, you say. It is both a self-touching and a projection.

Like all language, you feel it between your head
And the world that rolls unendingly before you
As you chase across the rug, slapping it out of the way.

While you are crawling, you can pretend to be the dog
Who fascinates you. But surely preference must be given
To the tall Da who makes you fly? A puzzle!

Down from the ceiling, twisting to get to the rug again
To be that rough one, you briefly brush the mouth that is
    like yours.
Now, think of all the words you can say standing up.

4 Radio Baby

Beneath the eaves they are talking to their mothers
And their mothers are talking, too, with pacifying voices
Over systems of alarm that accidentally connect

Speaker to speaker, from nursery to bedroom
And from house to house, the length of Tunley Road.
What can a baby have to say to a mother who is not his
    own?

It's a busy wavelength that will blur like this,
Thinner than an eyelash darkened with tears.
It is the kinship of blood, like a year of fine wines.

But a mother knows the voiceprint of her own child,
Knows it in utter darkness, in her sleep of remembered
    maidenhood,
In the silence of communication and in the chatter of dawn.

This is Radio Baby you are tuned to, Radio Baby!
With all its regular programmes, its clatter and announce-
    ments.
Its easy quizzes. The laughter. The audience participation.

5 Drums at the Tooting Durbar

M'Lord's carriage has stalled in the grass, in the commons.
Shall there be dancing to entertain him?
Shall they entertain him, the dainty kings and queens?

What's this, a dog? Oh! Oh! But it's unbelievable!
The freedom, the roughness of utterance! And the colours
    in the sky.
The strolling in no direction. The sizzling sweetmeats.

What is the difference between a drum and a balloon?
A balloon is large enough to head-butt through the grass
At the pace of a controlled scamper. A drum is a sound.

The drums speak the language of a nodding procession,
Hips turning, fingers pointing, fingers fat with rings,
Whole bodies edging along, half queue, half conga.

The drums speak the language of golden crowns,
Bent knuckles on the skin, dabbling the cheeks of the drum,
The sound filling the fragrant afternoon like a fountain.

Piano Concerto

Mikhail Pletnev at Angoulême

He takes the even steps of the resolute prisoner
Entering an arena of prepared discomfort.

He offers himself as for a half-portrait,
Turning slightly in the attentive light.

Do we expect speeches? He is silent.
He needs to earn our blessing still.

We have come for the confessions
That only pain can finally extort.

We want to hear the challenge of the forbidden,
The chattering of dissent, the stubbornness of heroism.

We want to hear the emotion
That belongs to the solitary truth.

We want to applaud the heretic.
We need this excuse for an old debate.

The instruments are held carefully
For they have been primed and charged.

The inquisitors look elsewhere:
Not one of them is less guilty than he is.

And now he takes his place, bowing his head.
And the instruments are raised. And it begins.

It is as we knew it might be:
The truth is not solitary, but an understanding.

Finally we know we are of neither party
But are impartial witnesses.

Out of the half-open black book of his torture
He reads the legends of joy in red and gold.

Their narrative is reflected in his cheeks and jaw
Which lift and tighten to control their uncertain hopes.

His fingers recreate the text as a river
That floods its black shores to conclusion.

There is, after all, nothing to defy.
He merely meditates upon its own laws.

Who suspected that these sublime proposals
Had once been made by authority itself?

Which now answers them in its own manner,
Turbulent, generous, bitter, enriched?

Behind his closed eyes there may be intuitions
Of which we can only appraise the translated fragments.

That his little problems in logic might have puzzled a child
Is our wonderfully encouraging conclusion.

And so they might be forgiven, as a child is forgiven,
Who then will jump and sing past bedtime.

Jump and sing until the ceiling thunders
With the moral happiness of justice done.

The noises we make in response are shouts of pure delight.
The execution was faultless.

Mosaïque Macaronique

Interlocking circles seek
A teasing labyrinthine plan
A travers le Basilique,
Un pavé cailloutis romane.

Galets lisses de Saint-Pierre,
Blancs et noirs, ils s'entremêlent,
And we ourselves are walking there,
Treading the shapes of Heaven and Hell.

Dim penitential voices bless
The soaring vaults with F in alt,
Mais sous les pieds de nos faiblesses
Sont cailloux polis de basalte.

Austère Mosé et Saint-Pierre
Se rencontrent en mosaïque,
Stone on stone established where
The law itself is a mystique.

A grown cathedral can be seen
As something larger than a cairn.
Ses carrés rouges comme nougatine
Coupés des volcans de l'Auvergne.

Parfois dans le Basilique
Le basilic comme hypnotiste:
Mountains are where the guilty seek
Interrogation of the Beast.

The walls delight in the grotesque;
God has a righteous chase in view.
Démembrements animent les fresques;
La voûte dévoile un Absolu.

Le samedi chez le Basilique:
Parfum de basilic, tomates.
Stalls along the pavement reek
Of all that haunts the human heart.

Every earthly thing we risk
Eternity to smell just once:
Odeur de la jeune odalisque,
Le sensualité d'encens.

Le Train Malin

This is my train song as it rattles through
Lullabaloo—lullabaloo,
The chestnut trees beneath the blue
From Corte to Aiacciu.

The cheeky little train that runs all day
Lullabaloo—lullabaloo,
Ultramarine and café-au-lait
Up to the mountain, down to the bay.

The track on its sleepers is a kind of stair
Lullabaloo—lullabaloo,
That curves and tunnels everywhere,
Depth for height, water for air.

In studious Corte all the bells sound hourly
Lullabaloo—lullabaloo,
Above the green-bronze shape of Paoli,
Dignified, but striding sourly.

They found him in the ancient citadel
Lullabaloo—lullabaloo,
They locked up Reason in a cell
And stopped the tale it had to tell.

The granite of the head must play its part
Lullabaloo—lullabaloo,
And yet the sea is where we start,
The ready motions of the heart.

The train hoots loudly as it now descends
Lullabaloo—lullabaloo,
Clearing the line, taking the bends,
Knowing that its journey ends.

Rivers are dry and pebbly in their beds
Lullabaloo—lullabaloo,
Piglets are squealing in their sheds
And the slow cyclists turn their heads.

A pair of horses standing tail to tress
Lullabaloo—lullabaloo,
Who never heard of faithlessness
Or felt they needed to impress.

And from the window what at last we see
Lullabaloo—lullabaloo,
Is nothing but the place that we,
Being not there, had wished to be.

Aigrette Garzette to Echasse Blanche

Follow, follow, white shadow
With nowhere to go.
Row over the empty air!

I am the guardian
Of the black bulls,
Snapper of libellules!

I am appointed
To whip the bounds,
To apportion duties.

You will never reach
The vision that I have
Of the earth's ending.

You are nothing at all, a copy
Of your reflection
In the flooded fields.

A blank eye
Wearied of wandering,
Easily startled.

You want to be like me,
Sharing the stirred reeds,
The ruses of horizon.

You perch at a distance,
The beak embarrassed in feathers,
Explosions of laughter.

. . .

Rivers push the land into the sea,
Trickle of waters,
The lagoons ending in fire.

Ever and forever a shadow
With nowhere to go.
Row over the empty air!

Madame Furet

Madame Furet on her whirlwind visit
    Has much to tell,
Banging at cupboards that will not open
    (Just as well),
Nosing at bags, fruit-stones, fruit-rind,
    Ends of bread,
Lifting her head to a table, diving
    Under a bed:
'When you may well in a year or two
    Be much vexed
To wonder further than the breath
    That is your next
And not impossibly your last,
    Remember me
Who live entirely at such moments,
    Free and unfree
By virtue of my breeding close
    To hopelessness,
That hedge-home where comfort has
    No known address.
I give you one brave look, as though
    You were a god
Whose only carelessness, to leave
    Crumbs where you trod,
Were too painful a puzzle for solving,
    As though square caves
Were hunger's heaven, defining the space
    In which the slaves
Of cornerless Nature are translated
    To emperors,
And the emptiness a mystery
    Daunting to us
But truly a required adventure,
    A threshold crossed
In despite of danger to my kind
    And the sky lost.

But, shadowless, you do not move.
          In your eye
Is a surprise of recognition.
          Let me pass by
Before you find me quite at home.
          Be still in surprise:
Give me time to be gone
          Or otherwise
Yourself turn from our encounter.
          You will have time
To judge, with humour if you will,
          My little crime.'
Bow-legged, one wave from ear to tail,
          She scampers past
With a panic skitter on the tiles,
          Moving fast
For green and safety. And the cease of speech.

Ratatouille at Villanova

Pepper, tomato, pepper and oil,
Onion, aubergine, onion and parsley,
Olive, courgette, olive and salt.

The bitterness of gourds in the richness of oil,
The ease of the heart in the savour of earth,
The openness of spirit in the fruit of the garden.

To eat on a terrace is to be welcomed back
As minor characters to the lost play of our lives,
Careless of outcome, knowing we will not change.

The sun moulds the oilcloth to the table
Like a painter casually preparing a canvas
For a study of nature he knows will make him famous.

Sea heaves its marble and sky is perfectly empty:
A sprig of dry herbs in a pot casts a shadow of ink,
And ink writes nature back into its own surface.

We are appointed to visualise a noble history
Of our latest entrance into the air,
But know it will turn out a comedy of sorts.

Come to me, my Maillol, with your salad of kisses!
Come with the ratatouille, cold from the shadow,
Bathed in its own horizon, the potter's careful thumb.

Carghjese

L'anachorète hélas a regagné son nid.
Max Jacob

Carghjese! The lamps come on at evening
And all that we wish for through a long
Day distils to a disappearance,
To dusk and a soundless song.

A late sail makes for somewhere,
The bay as silent as a book.
It stands still at our attention,
But gets there as we look.

There is an ikon in Carghjese
By a Greek hand, which shows the night
Coiled and rebellious against
The celebrated light.

A hunched and galloping St George
Drills the Dragon in the head.
Through scrolls and arcs of golden air
The idle eye is led

Down through the lance which is directed,
With all a surgeon's swift decision,
At obvious evil, to the core
Of an intent precision.

There is a kind of darkness in
Such concentration. The mind
And these lilies lose their colour when their
Contour is defined.

Stare as we will, the sun is still
Moving too slowly for us. We
Are restless in its orange light.
It settles on the sea.

And the horizon moves through cinder,
Smoke and rose to reach that realm
Where water is the pit of stars
And the gaze drops from the helm.

Carghjese is the throb of a distant shore,
Windows of the town like a lit barque.
The solitary sun croons in his cell,
Victorious in the dark.

When I Am Dead

This is addressed to you
From an immaterial where,
A non-place that is nothing
But what is in your head
As my words assemble there.

I am that silent state
In which we make no choice;
Stillness holding no promise;
Darkness that is all present;
Image that has no voice.

I am a kind of fulfilment,
The last flame in a fire.
Unlike a proposition
I am both true and false.
I am what you desire.

I am a visitation,
Not the dripping ghost
Of some restless regret,
But something gladly encountered,
The thing you want the most.

I come to you in dreams
And you wake upon the kiss.
If even now we are haunted,
No wonder that we cherish
The love we already miss.

Like this, when I am dead
The words and shadows move,
Translucent as ever, candid,
Inconsequential, as if
There were nothing to prove.

And though we may reflect
Upon their evident lack,
Dreams tell us of portals,
How we can never say
We are never coming back.

We cannot dream in the past.
In dreams we may not touch.
And though we are astounded,
Waking we often claim
That they were nothing much.

Oh, but they are fields of joy!
We ask for little more
When the cold world calls us,
Anchor drawn from the prow,
Stern slipping from the shore.

And I have nothing to give you
Except this love I send
In dreams of your own creating,
The life that has no body,
The story that has no end.

Dreams

These peaceable hills have horses:
You hear them just across hedges,
Noses in interrogation
Nuzzling and nudging their foals.

Snorting and nodding the head
In the startled release of breath
That sends invisible plumes
To create a language of air.

Bolted down to their shadows,
Their muscles remember movement:
A shuddering of delight,
A flurry of tail and mane.

This field-family is guiltless
Of all romance and betrayal,
Of that conscious animal power
We exercise over each other.

And their unargumentative passion
Is simply the statement of life
That starts with a knock-kneed stagger,
The red badge of the birth-string.

Yet their labial hedge-sounds
Announce a familiar riddle
Which was spoken above our cradles
And haunts our every sleep.

It is always there unanswered,
As now, at dusk before dinner
When we take the garden steps
To the scurry and lisp of the Usk,

Trout-mothering river
But shallow over its stones
That speak an even more primal
Tongue of intense attention.

This half-light is a key
To the full knowledge of all
We attend to, all we intend
With our insistent questions.

The Men's Ward in moonlight
When one of two souls awake,
Trailing a bloody catheter,
Cries: 'Where's my wife, then?'

And his life that stands in the light,
The light that insists on the dark,
Holds both for a terrible moment
In a wailing sightless gaze,

As though a man in his pain
Must know where he casts his shadow
And why for an awkward season
He interrupts the light.

The moon mounts the mynydd
Needing nothing for itself,
Etching the tilted field
Like an expensive binding.

It needs nothing but its display:
The turrets above our pillow,
Our moments still together,
The scents, the long-lived river.

And the horses stand in the moon
As though what was always intended,
As though what was always meant,
Was to make their shadows new-minted.

They stand in the pitiless moon
As the sun stood over them,
And their noses stoop to the grass
Where their foals are at last asleep.

And so we, too, fall asleep,
Joining our mothers and fathers
In dreams, and in dreams of the dreams
That they must have dreamed before us.

The Birds

At dusk the trees on the headland
Became a theatre for sparrows.

Leaves lifted and were after all wings
In simmering attendance

Rising and falling and rising
In silvery displacement.

We could imagine no peace
In that excited restless roosting

Rather a response to the moon
Which had lighted the lofty boughs

And left them in dim silhouette
As a place of argument and play,

A thousand fluttering occasions
Of exhaustion and dream.

The darkness acquired the intensity
Of mind at its moments of awareness,

Many leaves little darker than the sky
And the birds louder than water.

Three for Prue

1 A Boy Writing

This solemn shrimp, poring over his slate,
Is as naked as the hope he embodies.

One knee is lifted to support the careful capitals,
As if he is ready to leap up from his stool in joy.

But for the moment he is caught in alabaster,
In a lucidity of concentration.

Writing gets no more serious than this,
The first slow act, the letters about to shout aloud.

And you, my dearest, who have the knowledge
At the very heart of you, often near breaking it,

You must know that this little putto has a meaning
For you alone, for all you have achieved

For children whose similar beauty is only damaged
By the slightest crack in the smoothness of the marble

And whose own exclamations of gratitude and joy
Are as eternal as sculpture, and as silent.

2 Two Kites

Yours is a ruffled red bird,
Mine a staring green eye and a tail.

You ride the wind and sing,
I sidle and weave.

Where did we come from
Before we went aloft, adventuring?

We had been cared for by a few who had known
The simpler energies of horses and candles.

Is this why we search for such elemental things?
Here we are; and there we were.

The world's a wild place.
We reach out as we can.

Weak struts, papery ribbons, a drum of thread,
And the hope of an afternoon of air.

The strings hum, unreeled from the chest.
When they cross, it is mine that snaps

Who cares who goes first, the sky so blue?
It is the humming, and the tug.

Your kite is steady above us.
Its flying shadow darkens the field.

The grass flickers at its passing.
The grass darkens and burns.

3 Primroses

An anonymous archangel called in to say
That the primroses we picked will last another day.

How many times have we bunched the stems,
Cradling the heads in a single leaf of their kind?

How many such small crowds of flowers
Have looked over their green glazed rim

As if to wonder what sort of a space they were in,
Blankly, as their yellow pales into cream

127

And the green at the centre is a forgotten dream,
An echo of that cold season before growing?

You who have been called to a great exploit of rescue,
To raise the flower on its broken stem

Know that this business of caring is the need
To restore an elemental touch.

These are like all your assisted children,
Who would certainly crowd if they could

With a similar reach and twist of the head
To smile their sweetest smiles for you.

Gathered by you along the winding hedges of your life,
Noticed particularly in their own shorter journey.

Sweetness out of ditches, cardigan smells,
Granny's smell, Edie's smell, the sweetness of memory.

Sweetness in your loose fist, the sweetness
Of following you down this ancient lane for ever.

Prologue and Epilogue

Those twenty years we lived before we met,
Long gone yet partly traced, like history,
Seem now discountable, mysterious,
Petty to be regretted as not shared,
As two paths through a thicket reach the same
Broad upland meadow with its untrod grasses
A feathery haze of red, a Corot trick
To lose the single tuft among its kind
And lead the eye to wander where the light
Has only brilliant remarks to make.

And if my own path was a thorny stumble,
Grateful to find an opening at last,
I hardly cared what opportunities
You'd had to choose between alternatives
Or where those led, or if it mattered to you.
The seeds have fallen now, the grass is flattened,
We've almost done our feasting in the sun.
Together we attend the earliest star
As to a strict instructor of our fate,
And know by now how to respect its tale.

It stands there in the evening sky, as always
Suggesting endings and continuations,
A point of closure that allows the next
Inevitable sentence to begin,
A single blast that notifies the squadrons,
The brooding horn that wakes concerted strings,
The constellations waiting for their darkness,
The heavens waiting for the world to sleep
And we to watch, as one by one the stars
Shape their cold oracles at our request.

The future and the past might well be here
If we could read them as they once were read
Two thousand years ago on terraces
Like this, in villas very much the same

129

Beside this restless, many-harboured sea.
And still we give them that ironic look
Which tries to make them somehow, in our vast
Belittlement, accomplices of sorts.
We introduce them, like the years themselves,
Into our shapely private narrative.

But always underneath there is this murmur
Of some lost language, almost translatable
Yet fraught with meanings never caught or shared,
Those random busy years our life escaped from,
The years I still can be resentful of,
Remembering the unrememberable,
And finding them as chastening in their way
As what we neither of us know, their final
Counterpart, the matching epilogue,
The twenty years we hope we still have left.

If history has always been like this,
Shaped only by our accidental myths
And flowing anywhere (as Hardy put it:
A roadside rill after a thunderstorm,
Turned by a straw, or tiny bar of sand)
Then should we care what shape our water takes?
Where it has come from? Where it thinks it goes?
Its greatest moments, and the most surprising,
Are what we dare to give the name of love,
The meeting of our tributary streams.

Ghosts

1

The fire, springing to wispish life
On yesterday's raked coals, breaks out
Into its yellow authentic shapes.

The radio is building a library,
Discussing 'big-boned' minuets
Over a second breakfast tea.

Rain for the moment forbids a walk.
The hillside grasses flatten. Sheep
Graze into the frame of the window.

This, then, is the moment to
Review the images I woke with:
Human shapes with the spirit gone.

Dreams already broken when
I folded your nightdress, understanding
That cartoon symbol of the departed.

The swooping spook that certain cupboards
And staircases allow to haunt
With resentment and unfinished business.

Itself insubstantial, it
Invests sleeves with empty gestures,
Deep hems with a power to float.

But mostly troubles us with simple
Melancholy, hugging its own
Knee-hump before a fading fire

Like the girl who was a woman
Before she was old enough to look
Further than her day of pain.

2

Is it possible? Suddenly arms
And hair in the dark passageway,
A touch, and a draught of cold air?

Or the rumour of shadows against lit windows
In empty cottages on a mountain
Where night and the rain are masterful?

We can only believe in what we believe
To have been absolutely worthy
Of being somehow recoverable.

Not ourselves, certainly, existing
Nowhere but in the imagining
Of such imagining and capture.

We think of those whom we still owe
Some gesture, those we would have liked
To know, those we knew best of all.

Or is it that we have translated
Our unique consciousness into
A wish to persist and to survive?

Perhaps we are both victim and visitant,
Willing and sensuous in both roles,
Willing and fearful, like a lover?

These are chairs where the dead have suddenly
Sat bolt upright in the realisation
At once of presence and transience.

These are the shadowed ceilings where
Dreams ceased at an unfamiliar
Noise and speculation began.

These are the unoiled doors opening
On to rooms where a new consciousness
Of brief tenure sharpened the shapes

Of furniture that changed tense,
Where time that was neither night nor morning
Clung to objects that were going nowhere.

It hardly matters who felt these things,
For they are what we know we share.
The connection itself becomes the ghost.

3

And then I remembered figures falling
Willingly, escaping death
Only by freely postponing it

To take a few more breaths of their
Planet's precious gases, high-risk
Commodity eighty floors up.

And they were neither graceful nor clumsy.
They were neither living nor dead.
For this moment they lost their names.

For this moment, turning as if
Recumbent, one leg crooked as if
Finding comfort in sleeplessness,

They became simply the transient forms
Of their deliverance from being:
Handlocked divers, impossible stars.

They were arms and legs and trousers,
Already emptied, already ghosts.
They had overstayed their body's welcome.

Their city had betrayed them. Alive
Still in our sleep, they are like the damned
Spilling from an altarpiece.

Somewhere there is always ash
That has no glow or stirring in it.
Only a wind, lifting its surface.

A wind that buckets and yells across
These hills, beyond the parish, beyond
The oceans, all around the globe,

And has no notion what it can
Be chasing, or why, except that they are
Something like our vagrant thoughts,

That live in one place for a while,
And it blows them onwards and is their
Tormentor, deafening our dreams.

Prescience

To mourn throughout your life
That unknown day when you
Wake up for the last time
Is quite impossible.
It will arrive when it
Decides to, and will not
Be denied, though it be
Painful and unannounced.

Still, we toy with this thought
And find the resonance
Attractive to our sense
Of the deep recklessness
Of all physical hopes
Which nonetheless rely
On celebration and
Calendar calculations.

No candles on a cake,
Unless a countback from
Your theoretical
Threescore-and-ten might serve.
No congratulations,
Since all you have achieved
Is a noted dwindling.
What a licence for gloom!

No presents: far better
A disburdening of
All earthly possessions,
A practised letting go.
And yet the unseen guests
At the non-existent
Party expect some words.
It is that kind of day.

Take the example of
Virginia Woolf, who
In 1941
Walked into the Ouse on
The 28th of March,
Thus forever putting
From her like a locked door
The fear of going mad.

On that very same day
A dozen years before,
With deathday prescience
She opened her journal
And her pen sailed over
The calm flowing of the
Page: 'I met Nessa in
Tottenham Court Road this

Afternoon, both of us
Sunk fathoms deep in that
Wash of reflection in
Which we both swim about.'
And then, with precision,
Wrote: 'Only in myself . . .
Forever bubbles this
Impetuous torrent.'

She continued thus in
1929:'I
Feel on the verge of some
Strenuous adventure.'
In 1930 (though
She was writing about
Her novel *The Waves*): 'How
To end . . . I do not know.'

The following year her
Nib broke the surface of
The ink: 'Arnold Bennett
Died last night' were its words.
In 1935:
'Spring triumphant.' And in
1937:
'I shall lapse into dreams.'

These were deathday speeches:
Gracious, though in places
Troubled; prophetic, though
Never balefully so.
Whatever you are heard
To say on your deathday
You may be sure that it
Will hardly be noticed.

In fact, no one will be
There to wish you many
Unhappy returns; no
Cards clatter through your box.
But make no mistake. Death
Will come one day, smiling,
With that shape you must guess:
The stone in his pocket.

Flea Market

Place de Jeu de Balle, Brussels

And there will never be a time
When we will go down in the darkness,
Waiting until the platform clears

To open the stiff doors of the last tram
To Silence, lifting our failing feet
And unwillingly replacing them

Until we reach that square of dispersals,
To see our own lives laid out
On the cobbles for the scavengers.

We will never weep to see our pathetic
Trophies laid out on newspaper,
Turned over by the toe of profit

Or still heaped in their cartons of haulage
Where nothing is thought to be beautiful
That cannot survive its ownership.

The things we liked are like the things
We did, kept by us and remembered,
But imperfect to the judicious eye.

Weaknesses like photographs,
Faces instinctively lifted towards
A supposed immortality.

Wounded plates preserved in the uniform
Of their fortunate brothers, loved music
Cheapened by pencil and blackened corners.

The things that are only what they pretend
To be for as long as one pays them attention:
Paper flowers, magazine parts.

Objects that tease by confusing the appetites:
The mammary jelly-mould, the mannekin
Corkscrew, the can-can casse-noisette.

The trophies from foreign shores and occasions:
The coloured sand, the Exhibition
Mug, the aluminium amulet.

What has always been said is also
True: you can't take it with you.
So let us establish a useful countdown

Like eating the contents of the fridge
Before departure, to the last undated
Egg, saved rice and dwindled caper.

Such were a satisfying meal,
Though frugal, and appropriate
To the condemned prisoners we are.

All these objects that we believe
Define us: they ache already with
Our love, and their forgottenness.

Air Raid

Autumn's a brute. The trees
Raise arms to ward off blows,
Twisting from side to side.

There's nowhere they can hide.
How unsuspecting once
They struck their attitudes

Of poise and lift, blessing
The bounty of the light,
Alive to their very tips!

These broken limbs are like
A retribution exacted
For their vain need of transcendence:

Uplifted wrists scattered,
Old elbows dangling
In streams, shoulders smashed.

The punishment is random:
The vulnerable birch
Ignored, the sturdy ash

Split to the bole, and twenty
Oaks picked out in the wood,
Hoping to be unnoticed.

You, and you, and you,
Yes, and you! Here
And there, where the wind passed.

Lying against the hill
The trees seem merely tired,
Glad to have given up.

Some reeling at an angle
With a clod of stones and roots
That might bob them back like a toy.

Some still carrying parts
Of themselves, the injuries matching,
Splintered stumps and sockets.

Some defeated by a gust,
Top heavy with ivy.
Throttled, they soon gave up.

Some with their fury of leaves
Crushed into the grass,
Stunned, unlikely to stir.

What will we do with them?
No forgetting the place
That they had made their own.

No concealment of loss,
No mending of wounds like these,
No heaving to the vertical.

No averting the eye
From damage. But in
The stillness, the saws are busy.

The Philosopher King

The arms of chairs appear
To have ideas about
How we should sit in them.

They want us to grasp each end
With whitened knuckles like
A stage Plantagenet,

To lean forward, musing,
Slightly to one side,
One elbow raised behind us

In a grave posture of judgement,
Of deliberative wisdom,
A finger stroking the lip.

But there's no one in front of us,
No slave, no supplicant,
No arrogant adviser.

Thumb moves upon the grain,
Eyes cast about the room,
Head leans gently back.

But still the arms of the chair
Remind us of a duty
To reach into our thoughts.

If our fingers touch each other,
Our forearms complete a diamond
For the cat to jump into.

If we narrow our elbows
And lower them to our sides,
We feel strangely diminished.

We shrink into the chair
As a victim shrinks, resigned
To execution or teasing.

In fact, the roles are reversed
And the philosopher king
Is almost confined to a corpse.

Quick then: our royal proposals
Must launch a brilliant era
Of unarguable truth

Before we fall back upon
Protest or complaint,
Or lachrymose last-words.

Happy

for Emily

1

The two hundred and six most difficult pieces
And all the missing lights are now assembled,
Proving at last the whole triumphant thesis
That what in sonar otherness resembled
A fleshly anagram is now a shape
Made manifest, a clue now finally
Its satisfying reason, sole to nape,
Tree of the spine and apple of the knee.

This warm celebrity tells us a thing
Or two, or three: when answers must be right,
How art is always public, and how mothers
Must give much more than artists when they bring
Their concept of the human to the light.
Why we are most ourselves becoming others.

2

Parted, and yet not parted. Nowhere to hide
But everywhere. This is the paradox
Of being where he never was, outside
Or inside, little spring of the living box,
Folded mechanism of surprise.
So the immediate applause is his,
Appearing now before our very eyes.
No wonder that he got here: here he is.

And yet dependent still, and still at rest
He's beached like Crusoe, damp upon your breast
As though the struggle of his voyage meant
Only to make this resting-place the same
Safe home, or like the object of a game,
Where touching, he remains in touch, content.

3

There is a mystery in these earliest days.
They have an air of aftermath, amounting
To time suspended, out of your daily ways.
They don't belong with those that you were counting.
Nor with the future of a life that seems
For now to be content with breathing well.
You wake to them as children long for dreams
Where all their wishes find a working spell.

And yet the day itself is sacred now
And will be much remembered. Think of how
The run-up to it so obsessed you, though
The date was still unknown. In years to come
The countdown will be his, and his the sum
Of blazing birthdays that will see him grow.

4

What was the face before it was assigned
These wild expressions that betray the will?
Where was the will itself? And where the mind?
We think the future is a shape to fill,
A cheque to write, a life to give a name,
As though not knowing it is like our knowing
All that we do know, really just the same
But like a debt with only interest owing.

And so our hope fulfilled is unaffected
In many ways by being long expected.
How strange it seems! For though we find the traces
Here and there of features we know well,
It is his own, a story he can tell
Over and over, his face among our faces.

5

His season opens like an opening door.
Outside the window trees bear on their arms
New leaves like napkins stiffly folded for
The banquet of the summer. On his palms
Are similar fresh creases, and like leaves
His fingers are unfolding. Blossoms fall.
The street resumes its life: a push-bike weaves
Its idle circles, joggers hold up a wall.

And from above come sounds of that event
He celebrates with arias of content,
His waking. This is the world that he must bless,
For you who make him happy in it know
That he could only be so, truly so,
In certainty of your own happiness.

6

This little man's the robber of your sleep,
Spending his own brown eyes like currency
Where everything is ruinously cheap
And what he sees a second time is free.
He wakes to look, and he will wake you too
To look with him. The more he looks, the more
You look as well, and often, looking through
His eyes, you see things never seen before.

Yourself included. Look at that colour, full
To the pupils, like two buttons ready to pull
You to him, fastening him to your gaze.
Round as the unscrewed bottle of brown ink
Or two Welsh teapots touching above the sink,
A welcome in their bellied umber glaze.

7

That sound of his! Not quite an exhalation
Defining joy, nor yet a breathing-in
That strangely turns into an exclamation.
Something between a shudder and a grin
That borrows some of the still air around him
And with a dipping head that makes it dance
Takes it into his throat, which to astound him
Returns it as a kind of utterance.

Is this how language starts, by accident?
Or did he choose the sound for what he meant?
And how does meaning know it has that choice?
He makes the sound again, and often. Surely
Feeling has found a form, and gently, purely,
Recklessly, has turned into his voice.

8

There comes into his face, as though across
A planet movement of the wind or tides,
A gathering, a being at a loss,
A troubling of the sky when the moon glides
From its concealing clouds, a realising
Of some required address, the resolution
Of an enquiry of his own devising,
A play of muscle that is its solution.

It causes something like itself to be
The bright occasion of becoming the
Convincing model of the shape it takes.
Another face, of course! And he relates
Its smile to some idea he imitates,
Since making faces is the game he makes.

9

And now he hauls himself up to your knee
As if a couple of feet makes any clearer
Those things he knows he can already see,
As if a room's horizon could be nearer.
Extended on his tummy like a seal,
He chirps, and gropes for purchase with his toes.
He cranes his neck, and then decides to feel
The carpet with his forehead, tongue and nose.

In either posture (elevated, prone)
He lets you know that he is on his own.
The effort is laborious and full-frontal.
Standing will follow from the being tall;
From being extended he will learn to crawl.
Viva the vertical! Hey, horizontal!

10

Where do the old gods go when they retire?
When velvet ropes define museum spaces
In front of obelisks once crowned by fire?
When names are unremembered, and their faces?
Not that they do not have their worshippers.
They do. Those who still see them, and who gaze
At them with interest, and unlike us
Count their own wisdom not in years but days.

We recognise this worship in his eyes
By something in their colour, depth and size,
Like windows on to lawns where if you waited
Long enough you might expect to see
The gods happy again, and quietly
Pottering in the garden they created.

The Emperor Felix

In the first year of his reign
The Emperor Felix composed
His famous hymn to the light.

Sought: the ready blessing of
His immediate ancestor
To rise from the couch of the night.

In the second year of his reign
The Emperor Felix visited
The four corners of his empire.

Measured: the heights and surfaces,
The location of useful resources,
The paces of pilgrimage.

In the third year of his reign
Figs were placed before him,
And bread, and milk and honey.

Favours: whimsical largesse
To the tasters of his food
And the two great cats acknowledged.

In the fourth year of his reign
His activity was marked,
The significant works begun.

Ordered: the transport of gravel,
Circulation of the terraces,
Enumeration of flora.

Historians are uncertain
About the middle years
Of this illustrious reign.

Legend proposes the descent
Of an all-encompassing slumber,
A cessation of enquiry.

How then to account for
The beating of the stone drum
And the heroic investigation

Of that murmuring surface
Which second by second betrays
Its resistance to the horizontal?

How may we accommodate
The richly varied achievements,
The cautious calculations,

The staggering collection
Of objects whose precise use
Is to this day uncertain?

During his reign his shadow
Fell in every direction.
He was tireless, and worshipped.

He was carried everywhere
At his pleasure, his demands
Promptly acceded to.

Long ago we abandoned
Our gods, in disbelief.
But him we still believe in.

Two Roads

The future man trots gamely
Into the first definable
Prospects of his life
No further than a flower
Or where the cat was
Or a familiar voice.

But then, as time goes on,
Horizons hold no fear.
The known is not enough.
The whole world exists
To be stumbled through
With whatever sprawling, or sitting.

And off again at a pace
That gives no sign of faltering
Or guessing at resting-places
But aims to cover the ground,
That route between Now and Now
Which is a continued delight.

Our own tired road is shorter,
Anchored as it is to Then,
Uncertain, as ever, of When.

Great-grandfather

Released at last from their own interests,
The generations pounce and leapfrog,
Having nothing better to do

Than to question their posterity
Or to rock unsteadily on stones
Across the wet places of nostalgia.

We take adjacent generations
Much for granted. Born from them
Or giving birth to them is enough.

We take them much like draughtsmen
To reach the vantage of our vision:
The daughter's son, the mother's father.

Or further, the mother's grandfather,
The grandfather's grandfather, squares
Beyond capture, where vaulting stumbles.

These are the unimaginable
Places where the game changes
And the living blood laps at its borders.

The dear ones who would love us if
They could, and who have never touched us,
Are troubled no longer by their progeny.

We have their jokes and illnesses,
Little rules by which our game
Continues to be understood,

But their lives and faces are motionless.
How shall we ever know them? How
Shall we cry across that absolute

That keeps them from us? For only we
Can hold out our hands in hope
Of grasping something more than shadow.

As my grandson said of my dead father:
'Well, when he's finished being dead,
We'll go to see him then.'

Insects

These sun-spirits please themselves
And please us, not least by being
Busy at what they are about:
The haste of gossamer, lacing
Side-mirror to window
Before the engine cools.
The dragonfly unwinding
In elastic uncertainty,
Hovering above a pool.
And this bird-headed thing
Whirring from its waist,
Sipping the mimosa.

I see how we could have believed
In sylphs and goblins, posting
To the four corners of the air
And ministering to the sleight
Of seasons, the disappearance
Of the sustaining day.
For insects have this sense
Of catching time on the wing
And outwitting it, and us.
They have surely come from somewhere
And are off again without
Pause, steady of purpose.

Though for the second that we see them
They behave like idiots,
Shame-faced, shambolic:
The fly wrings its hands,
Staring into mid-distance.
The bee falls from its flower.
Mostly the moth, clattering
At lamps, drowning in wax,
Fails fully to impress,
Encountered in the morning,
Still, on the bathroom wall,

A bivouac in snow,
The high heroics forgotten,
Stranded between peaks
Of impossible enlarging flight.

Perhaps it is this failure
That gives us the licence to
Refigure them as fairies,
Commanding in their whims
And bracing transformations,
One step ahead of time.
But touchingly clumsy, too,
As we are clumsy. Feckless,
Changeable, mistaken.
Shakespeare's Ariel knew
The sweetness of the cowslip
But wanted to be all spirit.
And Disney's winged nymphet
Going down on a daffodil
Or lazily stringing dew
Has the air of choosing a flavour
Or an accidental jewel
That reflects credit on her.

It is we humans who wish
To be admired, to be free,
When we know we are powerless.
We are so aware of alternatives
That we invent the gift of magic
Which lightly ignores them.
We would love to be so small
As barely to be seen, to fly
And to utterly change our shape.
This would be a fine distinction
To compensate for life's brevity
And its insignificance.

Iguana Days

We have seen this pebble before
Though three feet under. From year
To year it changes position.

The sea dwindles its contours
But not to my brief eye
In a mere decade of watching.

Stone keeps its secrets.
Its smoothness is a ruse
To content us with surface.

At the heart of stone is pure
Concentration, which life
Is foolishly in love with.

We believe that the stillness comes
From its exact possession
Of a truth that is lost to us.

    . . . . .

In the Wiener Museum,
The iguana enacts
Such stillness, elbows braced

And leaning forward into
Thought, years of reflection
Shaping its motionless grin.

It reminds us of Sutherland's Maugham,
Though there is not a trace
Of that creative arrogance.

Its skin has become stone,
The brain is a stone, finally
Empty of all anxiety.

To bask like this on stone,
Like stone: a century
Might pass before you move.

So we make our images:
The eternity of the pebble,
The monumental pose.

Out in the street sits Ferdinand
Raimund in the repose
Of his theatrical success.

The boulevards circle the city
As the mind deliberates upon
Its roaring purposes.

It is like the sea's eager
Auditorium, between
The curtains of dusk and dawn

And Raimund is now marble,
Inattentive to applause, finger
Forever marking his chiselled page.

Positions in Bed

Hand sandwich, cold shoulder, glued knees:
There are long times in the night when sleep
Induces some unrelaxing postures.
Settling into them seems sensible:
The lightly-crossed shins, one instep
Upon the other ankle-bone,
The arm across the chest, fingers
Cupped like an epaulette, the chin
Erect on the pillow, as if for shaving.
Or risking the supine snore-prone loll,
The knee crooked at an angle, an arm
Cradling the yearning furrowed brow.
Or striding, striding, taking up
Quite as much of the bed as one dares,
One wrist over the edge of the mattress.
All these are credible positions
Even when we find ourselves
Suddenly, irritatingly awake
And able, indeed positively induced,
To analyse them at leisure, fearing
To move and wake our sleeping partner.

How, then, should we seek our perfect
Oblivion? Much like a crusader?
Ankles crossed and praying hands?
Or coffin-style, perfect repose,
A horizontal sentry-box,
Promptly lying to attention?
The thing about these bodily
Dispositions is their limited
Variety and likely discomfort.
Really we need to lose an arm,
Acquire a three-way socket for
The ankles, a mattress-cave for the hips.
Consider: to compose the body
Is a necessary preliminary
To the nightly act of its translation.

Perhaps one morning we will find
Ourselves absconded from the body's
Weary roll-call, unreturned
From the wild encounters that we seek
And nothing left of us but posture,
The crumpled relic of restlessness.

Bicycle

Drifting through my head one morning
At 5 am, some memories
From 1947 or 8.

The lunchtime ritual at Miss 'aunder's,
Corned beef thinly sliced, cold,
With hot dumped mashed potato.

The two bland flavours competing
With their anomalous temperatures
For the ready favours of appetite.

Filing in behind our plates
Already sparely filled, water
In fluted jugs, quarters of bread.

Our uniform was mauve and green.
Miss 'aunder herself throughout the meal
Talked aloud on subjects of interest.

But what was drifting through my head
On such occasions? Was I already
Looking forward to my escape?

To ride precipitously down
The Blackheath vales, almost as steep
As quarries, slithery with pebbles of flint.

The paths scored with runnels dry
Of water, danger to launched bikes
As they slalomed the clumps of thorn.

Later I learned that the heath had many
Plague-pits, and the highwaymen
Once galloped over London's dead.

I tried to think of all the bodies
Needed to fill up one vale
Like a Lord Mayor's pie of whitebait.

I had seen Wernher von Braun
Attempt to re-open one: the crater
Was scattered with the jagged steel

As though a giant had been attacking
Beans, and the pieces were still hot.
There was nothing there, a pit of water.

And a single body lay nearby
Like a secretary asleep on the grass,
With a pram, which someone had set upright.

I had thought this incident somehow
Theoretical or inadequate, though
My bedroom bulb had bounced to the ceiling.

And I remembered the crowds and fires
Of the evening of victory, the shouting,
And the wandering, simply to see more people.

Now in peacetime, in mauve and green,
I listened to Miss 'aunder, doyenne
Of table-talk and mashed potato.

What did she talk about? Not death,
I think, nor the topography
Of death. Nor about bicycles.

Waiting

The little body I was in
Starred on the grass. While all around
The grimed yellow brick of London

Projected its iron balustrades
Into the theatres of unpruned garden,
Stalls of laurel, gods of willow,

With flinty paths on which my cats
Stood unconcerned as usherettes
And the clouds passing like scenery.

Gardens are the soliloquies
Of our agon with the authorial earth,
All morning interrogating worms.

All afternoon crucifying a tree
With an air-pistol, the silvery slugs
Studding the bark like slow typing.

I was still waiting for the scene to open,
Waiting for the downy-jawed girl
From the flat downstairs to come and play.

The lonely tangent of childhood locked
Into its slow ascent, the world
Bathed in the weathers of its future.

Too Late

Summer of all seasons in its core
We feel to be wasted. It has passed
Almost unnoticed, like happiness.

How early it began! Earlier
Than we had realised, not too late
It seems, to take it fully to heart.

The welcome of a wood suffused
With bluebells which we never saw,
The mating of thrushes, thickening grass.

These things occurred while we were waiting
For them to occur, and leaves made shade
That still required the sun to prove it.

The year's tennis star is crouched
At the service line of his career.
The ball is dripping from his hand.

The gum of the sycamore is suspended
Like aerial gossamer above
My pile of examination scripts.

We are booked like actors to appear
At the triumphant opening:
The leaves are a superfluity of tickets.

We approach summer like conquerors
Entering a city already ravaged,
Hollow stems and dried blossoms.

Scorched grasses with lines of ants
Like native bearers, spikes and thorns,
The reek of pods and seeded herbs.

The exhalation of the summer,
Its reach and perfect stillness, the sea's
Calm at the close of a sandy path

Bearing a dab of a white sail
Like a sudden excitement, all now
Forgotten, shut from the restless mind.

Now there will be no more of it.
Now pears bomb a vacant flower-bed
And garden wood is damp to the grasp.

Now we are in a mood to expect nothing
But the rich disappointment of the mood itself,
The heavy bending of a plant that is shed

Of its compulsions towards the receiving soil
And whose root now takes a grip of that dank chill
Even as its stalk springs lightly back.

Song

Yellow's the stubble of winter,
Yellow's the trumpet of spring,
The yawn of the tulip awakens
A throat that will sing.

The wine is the green of the summer,
The lime is the green of its leaf,
The scents of a season dissemble
The taste of its grief.

And now is a time of no colour,
The stem and the fruit are cut,
The branch is bare at the window
And lips are shut.

Freeze

Our normally effusive friend
Has nothing to say: he has dried up
Like an actor on a too-long tour.

That grave soliloquy into
The bath, that ready repartee
With the kettle: all utterly forgotten.

Ice-cube wit, lavatory humour:
Not even a splutter of protest.
It's his last gasp, horribly smothered.

His understudy is to hand,
Chattering away to himself
Out there as usual on the hillside,

So I'm off to teach him what I can
In my coat and muffler and grim cap
And a pair of buckets like a milkmaid.

Thank God for Nature when supplies
Fail us. I can write by sunlight
Though it will not bring me Handel.

The birds will have to do, although
In this deep stillness few are forthcoming.
They must be playing away this season.

The sound of my feet on the frozen ground
Reminds me I'd rather be eating biscuits
With the mug of coffee the tap denies me.

First things first, as the Master said,
So I sink and tug one dripping bucket,
Then the other, out of Wilbur

And admire for a moment, in the fall
Between boulders, the shapes of ice
In blebs and shanks and grassy knobs

And the long fingers that play upon
Their secret organ-pipes the quick
Voluntary of the stream.

Games

for Mick

Your boots are here, taller than mine
And with swish buckles, against your return.
Whenever I wear them I have a desire

To run on the spot with little steps
Like a substitute preparing himself,
Or to kick out at foxgloves, wildly.

I have emended the Rules of Cottage Golff
To take account of time's casual
Handling of this collapsing terrain.

Also in expectation the kitchen
Is laid with garage glasses and Jamesons,
And smoke already fills the rafters.

Alfred Tennyson is here, coughing
Over a fag, and counting out
Yellows and greens, and blues and reds.

Browning is shuffling all the packs,
Including the one where the nine of hearts
Is a brown vole from a children's game.

Alfred, soon writing IOUs,
Looks in the dresser for another
Bottle. He speaks extremely slowly.

'Lucky that cigarettes came in
Just as I was thinking of
Dear Ida and her fainting Prince.

They gave the thing a certain lift.'
Robert looks up and motions him
Back to the table: 'Come on, get dealt.'

'I have in mind,' says Alfred, 'an account
Of life as a perpetuity
Of warring graves, a diminishment

Lit only fitfully by eyes
Looking up in uncertain hope
From the pressed latch of the trysting-gate.'

'A hope too far,' Robert replies.
'Surely it is precisely there
That the betrayals proceed unhindered?'

The cards are dealt, and for a time
The world and its violence are redeemed
By smoke and abstract speculation.

Will you not join us? There is chocolate.
And, after midnight, five-card tricks
To be doubled. Re-doubled. And won.

And from the other room, the drone
Of pipes and swaying strings, wooing
Us insistently with song.

It is the poet Kangarova
With the catch in her voice and her derisive
'Yok, yok, yok, yok.'

She is known only to this hillside
In Wales, and because she sings for me
She will sing freely to all my friends.

And in the morning, if the weather
Allows, there by the door are standing
The rubber shapes of your restless feet.

Dusk and Dawn

In Mahabalipuram
We prepared for sleep, careful
Of the scuttling lizards.

When you suddenly woke
In the middle of the night
('We have to catch a taxi!')

It seemed appropriate
To a ready mode of moving
Between our plotted points

And I half believed you, awake
In a room reduced by darkness,
A refinement of uncertainties.

For I realised that the primitive
Air-conditioning had made
Me dream I was on a train.

There is a style of adventuring
And a delight in journeys
Which appeases life's anxieties

And this is their contained model,
Where any circumstance
May be hostile or benign

And all the world's treasures
Are never enough to ransom
An afternoon's heartache.

And I remembered Greece
In 1959
With an untroubled vision

Of our young bodies still walking
Together hand-in-hand
Through the heat and dust

As well, I suppose, they may
In some god's imagination
Even when we are dead.

We had our lives in prospect:
Innocent, wasteful, beautiful,
All that the young must be.

After forty years and more
We are what the old must become:
Resigned, cautious, hopeful.

It might be that we slept
Beneath the moon on Rhodes
And woke in this older land

Where the crickets at dusk
And the stoneworkers at dawn
Make a similar music.

Tapping at first light
In a regular syncopation,
Near, but invisible,

And far, and much further,
Strangely aware of each other,
On the beach, in the town,

And falling in and out
Of mysterious synchrony
That is like the music of marriage.

In Mahabalipuram
We woke as we have always
Woken, grateful for the day.

And our lizard friend was pinned
To the wall of our shabby room
At an angle, like a brooch.

from THE SPACE OF JOY (2006)

Coleridge in Stowey

*'Why we two made to be a Joy to each other, should for so
many years constitute each other's melancholy – O! but the
melancholy is Joy –'*

S.T. Coleridge

Wrestling the challenge of Infinity
To Personality, I sometime heard
The Bride's voice, distant, from her bower,
Less often now. I argue with my self;
Certain, therefore, of half a certainty
Before the mists assert their mistiness
And leave me without a Way.
                           And now at eve,
Where once beneath a sprawling tent
Of dappled leaves and aromatic keys and flowers
I set my creaking chair's unequal feet
Upon the bulging roots that sank down deep
Into green Somerset for sustenance,
It has become my wintry pleasure here
To find my self not in an obscure wood,
But somehow lost beneath a single tree
That like a cage lowers its naked branches
Towards the icy bareness of the soil.

Truly a prison that the season locks
As a mind is locked by thoughts that put it there!
Unfeeling, inward cogitations, blind
To the light that still streams from a chilly West.
The satisfaction of the solitary
Is to think to be defined by others' thoughts
Concerning him, enjoying their concern,
Relishing misery so long as he
Is made its object, like a Pietà.
The heron has the patience to be patient,
Though there be never a fish in sight.
Would he may not starve! And furthermore
It were unnecessary that the worm

Make friends; and therefore to its social sense
The convivial temper is unknown. I hail
These stoic fellow-creatures in my soul!
Heron, worm and poet share the doom
Of labouring for a scant reward!
                              Inside,
The coals burn thinly on their wretched altar.
The Shadow Folk on walls and ceilings, guardians
Of our quieter Selves that after kettle-quarrels
Settle to nodding by a flickering stove,
Make mocking Panoramas of such battle.
They are our little household gods, masters
Of a moment that undoes all painful knots,
Loosening shapes to fly like smoke and light
And makes our stillness move still, though still, in fancy.
For there is joy upon the cess of words
Spoken in heat, joy in admonishment,
Joy in the melancholy pilgrimage
Our staffs pace out in almost unison
Greater than joy itself.
                         And here is Hartley,
Little dear Heart, patient philosopher,
His palms clasped to his lips as if to mock
Some grave proposal, not of his usual play
But of a Voyage back to his beginning,
A novel understanding of his place
In the unfixed perplexing scheme of things.
I offer him a piece of cheese, entire
For the moment that its crumbliness allows,
And gladly he takes it as one who reconciles,
In gracious condescension, the Many with
The One.
            Our very first posterity
Is but a small parcel of infinite Joy
Troubled only by the animal spirits
Which went into its making, and our wonder
At the hysteroplast is but a glimpse,
A memory of our own origins,
Grieving with a full heart that such fresh Joy

Will soon become a Melancholia
Like ours.
                    The woman gives him a bowl of soup
As though he were not mine and certainly
Not hers, but as though my many faults had left him
The better deserving of such charity.
I am to her merely a child, as he is,
Our occupations equal as separate play
In the one chamber.
                    His cheese falls in the soup,
And I talk with the Shadow Folk to tell them
The Mountains of the Moon are like the veins
In cheese, or embers of a fire, that make
Faces of our present disposition
Out of old satisfactions. And I think
Of him in his first slumbering stillness where
Feeding with ruddy cheek against the moon's
Blue vein-of-a-mountain, the new god's
Baby feet twitched in clouds of linen.

Enthusiastic in his saintliness,
The bridegroom ordered harps, which rendered praise
To him for his forgetting lamps, and now
All that I say is what I know is true,
Though with a bitter voice that may be challenged
As the unspeakable, irrelevant
To ears that have no need to hear it, and thus
One with the freezing blast that rises now,
Rattling the branches of its cage. O most
Miserable! O vain shadow of shadows!
I have seen the depth of shame, the bride weeping.
I have, outrageously, spoke my own sentence,
And our triangulation, like the new maps
Commissioned by the Ordnance for the War,
Creates a blankness in the living world
That may not be traversed.
                    All evening
I sit in the parlour in my great-coat like
Satan hiding wings . . .

Brahms in Thun

Who is that singular man upon the path
Winding from Hofstetten, his long black coat
Greying with age, the shawl over his shoulders
Fastened with a pin? The flannel shirt
Collarless, and the shabby leather satchel
Surely full of bohemian mysteries?

The urchins know who he is. He shoos them away
With the hat that's always in his pudgy hand.
The girls know who he is. When he draws near,
A trifle corpulent, full-bearded, grey,
They notice with a flutter of the heart
The piercing blue eyes of a younger man.

Who certainly notices them. He gives a bow,
A brief acknowledgement of what their eyes
Have searched for in his eyes. Then looks away.
This is not the time, nor ever will be,
For words to rob the unspoken melody
Of its elusive and absorbing fragrance.

It haunts him now. Its cadences arrive
Like the brief mysteries of flowers in spring,
Frail for the buttonhole, their scent soon gone.
But now in the dust of summer let him stand
And let the petals open, let them fall
In all their fullness to the reaching hand.

This morning, stepping from the deep-eaved villa
Rented from Herr Spring, half in its shadow,
He paused just for a moment, lit a cigar
And breathed at once the air and its aroma.
This is the mood of amiable resolution,
The piano as portico to an adventure.

He feels that he might stroke the Wellingtonia,
Whose roots beneath the hill drink in the lake,

While here by the railings at megalosaurus's height
Its branches stir in their Jurassic calm;
Stroke its rough hide as if it gave off sound,
As if the pine were strung to its very tip.

Even now the smoke continues its
Vague dispersal through the shadowed tree,
Lofting minutest particles in the warm air
To the pine's pinnacle, where the needles cease.
Although now he has passed along the path,
The stride determined, tobacco in clouds about him.

The tiles of the Thunerhof below are severe
To the meditative eye, the circular divan
In the Bellevue salon equally distracting.
There the Knechtenhofers' assembled guests
Would eat the famous composer half-alive
To occupy the lateness of the morning.

'Milord Ponsonby would wish that he
Were here, as we ourselves are glad to be:
The great artist in sounds, the sheet of the lake
Covered with quavers of sails, a glass or two
To toast Vienna and to hear a tale
Of Elgin, ruins, and a grand concerto . . .'

A lion, then, among the jackals who
Would lift their jaws from working, prick their ears
At rumours of a richer feast elsewhere
And leave their crumbs of carrion behind
For the bored waiters of the Speiseterrasse.
Take heart: the Bains de Bellevue are not for him.

On, on, to the Schüssel in the Plätzli,
The beer ingratiating, dizzy and blond,
The company reliable, with shouting laughter,
The schnitzels overlapping their plates all round,
Heavy as dewlaps of long-slumbering hounds,
The flower fading on the creased lapel.

But in the mind, where flowers never fade,
There lives one favoured face that is a smile,
A smile that is a voice: '*O komme bald*!'
'Come soon, come soon! Before the May winds blow,
Before the thrush sings in the wood, oh come!
If you would see me once again, oh come!'

The voice is hers, and yet the song is his.
Who can be certain where the yearning lies?
Her lips are parted, and his notes come out.
Her throat swells with the thrilling melody
That will make others weep; so she and he
Survive their shout of grief, inviolable.

But is it grief? Not joy, perhaps? She gave
Him joy. He gave it back as if it were
Some sort of tender, self-inflicted wound:
'Often in my dreams I hear you calling,
Calling outside my door. But no one wakes,
Nobody is awake to let you in.'

What does he think they mean, these words?
Fate is in them, also resolution.
Death, too, is there, and also a wild hope:
'Come, then, for one last time, for you will find me
Gone from a world that has no place for us.
But if you come, oh if you come, come soon.'

And will one come again, will such a one?
His Fräulein Spies, the charming Rhinemaiden,
Herma, Herminche, Hermione-ohne-o?
He follows her to Wiesbaden, full-tilt
At his Third Symphony, sets Groth for her.
He's never in his life written so fast.

And he'll produce her for the Widmanns (guilty
Of curiosity about the work
She has inspired). Rigorous torture by song's
Their punishment: the jovial composer

And his Krefeld songstress will come to them with skewers
('*Spiessen und Stangen!*') next Wednesday after dinner.

Wonderful Thun . . . . The steamer on the lake
Hoots at the afternoon; its paddles ply
The Aare to the harbour where he sees
Such parasols in clusters, greeting, retreating.
Beyond, a train is puffing into the station
Like an old gentleman expecting treats.

Later he might allow himself to walk
Down there again, a brandy at the Freienhof,
And in the Markt the smell of girls and herring.
And will one come again, will such a one?
It haunts him like something about to disappear.
He tries to put a name to it, but fails.

Perhaps it is something he has always missed,
The sound of laughter in another room,
Hands at his knee, hands tugging him away,
The playing, the watching, the kissing and the dancing,
The faces echoing their other faces,
That strange projection of the self, like art.

Some melodies are statements like the mountains,
The Stockhorn, Niesen, and the Blümlisalp,
Claiming their definition of the sky,
Others elusive as the mist which rises
Like half-remembered dreams from the still lake
In which the sky and mountains have been drowned.

And they exchange their notes in playful ways
That echo all these harmonies of nature
Where one thing, though itself, reveals another:
Fields broken by trees, forest by pasture,
The levels of the Aare linked by weirs,
Its course shaped both by broken land and water.

The little town itself, with its red roofs,
Rises like a flowering of the earth,
A human watchfulness that celebrates
The parting of the river from the lake
In boyish determination, that sees its future
Clear, and makes its watery business there.

And the Schloss, its profile out of fairy-tales,
Throws up its pointed turrets at the sky,
Casements of trance, imprisonment or longing
Where distance is for once the only meaning,
Its central slab of tiles uncannily
Matching the Stockhorn like a falling cadence.

And will one come again, will such a one?
And what on earth would happen if she did?
Herma, Herminche, Hermione-ohne-o,
The voice embodying the melody,
The melody abstracting from the heart,
The heart enchanted by an opening mouth.

'I am a man who's getting to those years
Where he quite easily does something stupid,
And so I have to doubly watch myself.'
And Clara thinks she's being left in the cold,
Dear Clara, arbiter, his earliest muse,
Old lady at the keyboard in a cap.

Who, when her darling Robert in his slippers
Left her and ran out through the carnival
To throw his person into the Rhine and madness,
Preserved herself for music and her children,
Year upon year preparing for her concerts
Like a devoted priestess at the altar.

Who taught him out of tragedy to know
That feelings are firmly locked within the stave
Lest they uncover foulness: what would she say?
The fingers scramble like waves upon the shore,

Tides of regret advance to their conclusion,
Storming their beaches, where her profile bows.

There are mistakes too terrible to be made,
When to approach them, as to an upstairs room
Where light invites the idle passer-by,
Is to stand upon a brink of fascination
Whose logic is a desecration and
Whose music is a series of farewells.

All that this art in its bodily abstraction
Has seriously learned to do: to exult in pain
And be stoical in pleasure, to be triumphant
With propriety and reserved in ceremony,
To take grief into fury and out of it again,
He had for long with mastery acquired.

His mood now is a matter of resolution,
Where resolution has no certain hope
To pronounce an equal love impossible
In waves of thunder shot with trickles of light,
To embrace the damage of the soul with joy
And to erect the architecture of tenderness.

His hand moves over the page like a flock of birds
Seeking rest in snow, their tracks a relic
Of the enduring passage of a hunger
Across an infinite waste, a fragile heartbeat,
The Stockhorn, Niesen, and the Blümlisalp,
At once forbidding and familiar.

Quick, catch their flight . . . The hand continues to move,
The quavers swarm, the sheets fall from the piano,
The rhythms fight it out, the prey's in sight,
Crisp noble chords, the strings making decisions
That their invisible fingers lead them to,
The next idea that lies in wait for them.

The only respite is a dark Kaffee.
The ritual itself is stimulating:
His brass pot from Vienna with its spigot;
Its porcelain stand; the little burner moving
Its blue flame like a crocus underneath;
The grinding of the Mokka from Marseilles.

And a cigar, of course. And in its wreaths,
The music for a moment laid to rest,
He lives within the mood it has created:
And will one come again, will such a one?
And what on earth would happen if she did?
How to accommodate that bodied voice?

Herma, Herminche, Hermione-ohne-o!
Is it too late? Isn't the paradox
Just this: the one mistake committed is
The one that will transcend both fear and error
And in its act be no mistake at all?
And will one come again, will such a one?

Somewhere in his mind the names proceed
Like cases that have come to shape a law:
Clara, of course, Agathe, Julie, Lisl,
And all the singers of his Frauenchor
Whose voice and beauty caught his ear and eye,
Music's muses, music's priestesses.

They ring him round with their accusing looks.
He kneels before them in contrition, asking
Of song if the perfection of its moods
And of its utterance has power to
Redeem the soul of a defective man.
And song, as usual, has no sort of answer.

Nor does Kaffee. And nor do Frau Widmann's buttery
Plum pastries. Nor does the Wellingtonia.
Nor does that broad and energising vista
Across the lake where paddle-steamers ply,

The Stockhorn, Niesen, and the Blümlisalp,
Each reassuring as a reputation.

For there it is. The music must be written.
And Fräulein Spies will have her début in
Vienna. And Karlsgasse num. 4 is only
An old bear's den, almost a hermit's cell.
And the Bernese summer, like every summer since
The beginning of the world, will soon be over.

And with the summer over, who can say
What may be found in the satchel of mysteries?
Wonderful Thun . . . . The watchful fairy Schloss,
The midwife of his own late blossoming,
Herma, Herminche, Hermione-ohne-o,
The Trio, the Sonatas, and the Songs.

'Come, then, for one last time, for you will find me
Gone from a world that has no place for us.
But if you come, oh if you come, come soon!'
The instruments inscribe their own enticements
Upon the holy movement of a heart
Too long alone to know when it is teasing.

'It comes to me, this thing, whatever it is,
Like the spring flowers that steal upon the senses
And drift like scent away. Then comes the word
That holds it before my eye until it pales
Like the grey mist, and like a scent it dies.
Yet still a tear calls fragrance from its bud.'

That tear is music, emotion's memory,
And God forbid there should be story in it.
The good Herr Doktor with the forget-me-not eyes
Strides on, the emperor of a world of sound
So pure he scarcely sees that its grand truth
Is fatally wedded to the human voice.

Wallace Stevens at the Clavier

I

I am the amateur of tragedy,
The Knave of Hearts, the Quince of Ives,
My fingers laddering the ivories,
Idly chromatic, quintessence of white and black,
White of the inner thigh, the black of lace
And all that jazz, the hootchie-cootchie-coo.
Why play the Concord Sonata if you could
Play Chopin, or both, or Chopsticks for that matter?
For music is apprentice to desire,
To yearning, or the comedy of kisses,
Here at this keyboard, thinking of wanting you.

II

But music has no pages. It expands
To fill the empty spaces where it plays
Like any calculated melancholy.
And memory agrees with Meredith
That we inhabit all that we have done,
Inhabit the idea of it, which is
The parent fountain of our deepest life,
Opposed to that of perishable blood.
Then let, out of the fury of our fingers,
Something like a melody be heard
Beneath the stabbing of a tenor thumb.

III

Too late, exclaims the Spoiler of Satisfactions!
But even at this moment there's a hope,
Like the false gleams of sunset that distil
Easy beneficence across a lake,
That all defeat may be postponed, that night
Might just reserve its absolutes for once.
Pages of Brahms that say so come to hand
With all their loving dedications and
With all their folded blackened corners, locus

Of an ecstatic passion hymned as it departs
In half-acceptance of imagined loss.

IV

The piano steers into the summer falls,
Floating through cresses and blue butterflies,
The music of an idle voyaging,
Portrait of a girl in a chapeau
That might have graced the lake at Fontainebleau.
I push the pole and steady in the stream
Of melody, its tink-a-tink-a-tink,
Canoe canoodlings, all those forgotten things.
My foot treads on the Bechstein's creaking step
As if to hold the evening from its fall.
The page is ending with a double bar.

V

You might reflect, as fellows often do,
On inch-thick cold roast beef and English mustard,
A bold adventure for an afternoon!
Viburnum springs back from the fingers but
Its scent remains. In navy, white and grey,
The geese compose a print in Japanese
With questioning necks attendant in splayed feathers.
And should the sun be parsimonious,
Reminding us of summers lost, no matter.
Since summers once existed, let us go
Over to the Canoe Club to make hay.

VI

I turn to Opus 118, A Major,
Andante teneramente, opening with
Three wistful notes like fingers reaching out
That find no other fingers but describe
An airy gesture of their own, which says:
I have no otherwhere to turn but here,
C sharp, B and D, interrogation,
Reflection, memory, hope and regret.

These are my mood's containment. They expand.
They stretch. And fall back into rumination.
Too late? Too late! Yet, not perhaps too late.

VII

C sharp, B and D; then C sharp, B
And A: a lifting of the little phrase
That signifies some sort of faint resolve
Embodied in the awkward reach of fingers.
Now this is truly Elsie, truly you
As once you self-expectantly became,
Waiting in Reading for my New York letters,
An intermezzo in a greater opus
Peculiar to that suspended state,
Pellucid opuscule to make us blink,
A glimpse into the rawness of the heart.

VIII

Now I can read my poems as I read
This music, as a pure recall of feeling,
Finding in their notes some thoughts of you,
A kind of thinking of thinking of wanting you,
Not as you are, but as you were composed
By that impulsive hand that is first love
Tracing in fitful touch the sound of shape,
The shape of beauty that is in the mind.
The memory that falters in the fingers,
The fingers that press down upon the keys
Like the great roots of trees, slaking a thirst.

IX

The piano is a threshold that will bring
Beauty to its imperishable heaven.
Here is an eye the straying fingers say,
And *one by one, the lashes of that eye*
In cadences like modesty, or flashing fire,
Until the whole assembly in the mind
Is she herself, the true Badroulbadour!

If once it was mortality I feared,
As I imagined her a prey to worms,
Now it is time's indifference, the slow
Ceasing of an enchantment, and long silence.

X

The comeliest girl in Reading, Pennsylvania,
Entirely blonde and pale, a childlike skin,
Wearing the biggest hat you ever saw:
Who would not weep to fail to win her hand?
I have seen lesser marvels that were wronged:
The one false note that habit likes to play,
Rugs soiled, wild lemons left to rot.
If life were perfect, then we might declare
That there is nothing in the scale of things
To cause such grief, as this bleak aftermath:
To treat a wife as if she were mere ash.

XI

The worms consume only the accidence
And must themselves be numbered for her name
As though it were the answer to a riddle,
The single thought of her, *out of the tomb:*
Badroulbadour, we bring Badroulbadour.
But ah, the substance: that is poetry,
That pours reality into the mind
Like an extraordinary cabernet,
A cabinet confined of cabernet
Left for the dozen years it needs to be,
Left for a married lifetime, if needs be.

XII

Aladdin hidden in the hammam knew
The singing of the blood inside his head
That shamed the elders to accuse Susannah,
But his Badroulbadour was truly blameless
And bore her body ceremoniously
Among her maidens to the secret bath,

A little moon outshining a host of stars,
A moon unveiled as unimagined sunlight,
The spells upon her cheek with a burnt rose
Teaching him conjurations of desire
And shattering for ever his repose.

XIII

Who could have thought such beauty as he saw?
A veil was lifted from his eyes and he
Was good for nothing and he knew no rest.
His head was music and the music silk.
And everything was changed inside his head
By what he had not known to be outside it.
This was the world of all the possible worlds,
Standing in its uniqueness, shadowless.
This was the earth he loved enough to die.
His mother wept for the stone of her heart's fruit
And for her boy's ambition, and its object.

XIV

What, if we are gifted, is that gift
But consciousness that we might give again?
As the young poet, dreaming in violet cities,
Gives back to villages their consciousness
Of wonder and invisible esteems.
As the poor lover, pacing the lonely streets,
Bids the Ifrit of his imagination
Describe for him a palace of desire
In which his love might live, as he has lived,
In the abstractions of a fictive night
That turns all light to fathomable sound.

XV

Aladdin was a tailor's son and knew
How to sit cross-legged in humility,
A shearsman of sorts, plying a simple craft
That clothed the world with his imagination,
Graced in good fortune to become a god,

As poets are who conjure palaces
And other worlds for beauty to inhabit.
The birds that flocked about its turrets cried
Humiliating cries of their raw needs
And melons rotted in untended gardens
And the world declined as the blue music played.

XVI

The bridegroom's music is a spectral waltz
That severed fingers play in shuttered rooms
After another day has done its stuff.
I have torn off too many calendars
To claim a quiddity in certain bones
That let a person jig, or not, at will.
We are automata who turn and turn
Until we stop and pray ourselves to peace.
And yet I lie, waiting until the day.
Apart from me, shut in the robber dark
The music suffocates beneath its lid.

XVII

Throughout the night I tried to dream that you
Were once again beside me, and you were.
You lay in perfect weight and quiet breathing,
Famous and private, my familiar.
And yet throughout the night I was alone,
It being, after all, only a dream.
The lamp that won you, that you gave away,
The lamp, the lamp is truly lost, the palace
Disappeared that housed Badroulbadour.
If somewhere it exists it is not here.
If somewhere you exist I am not there.

XVIII

We live together in the house, apart,
One side the womenfolk's, the other mine.
Walls are no hindrance in a garden where
You'll find a variety of lilies and

A giant white rabbit that is eating them.
A heavy man is strolling beneath his thoughts
And thirty-cent cigar smoke out of Tampa,
Reflecting on the freedoms of the place,
The conversations in the evening air,
The memories of decisive secateurs
Or Holly nude in the magnolia tree.

XIX

Of roses on the piano, by her hand
Cut and displayed, is little to be said.
They are the young god fallen into sleep,
The lacrimae of some outworn amour
That throws a truculent scent into the air,
The faded cousins of an adjutant brandy
Placed to excuse the pianist's rapt mistakes.
They are the moving mezzotints of nature,
Against which sound proclaims eternity
In its grave absolution from a pain
That rises from the keys into those roses.

XX

When Adolph Weinman came to look at you,
You were not thirty. Immortality
Was in his gift, like the assassin's knife.
His Liberty beside the rising sun
With sheaves, his aviatrix Mercury,
Close-helmeted, erect, scanning horizons:
These were the coin of the new century,
The ikons of a need that strode the world.
O woman with the hair of a pythoness,
You are the profile of a currency
Placed in the palms of beggars like a blessing!

XXI

Your nose is spared from sharpness by the touch
Of many ignorant fingers, and your cheek
Faded to an unnatural smoothness, ghostly

Upon the familiar features of your face.
You flit like Mercury from soul to soul.
When once I spread my gems of marvel out
Like fruit upon a dish, and saw you take
Your fancy there, as you might twirl a fan,
You lead me to the understated darkness
Of this dead room, where on a dresser of deal
I heap my loose change like cold memories.

XXII

Dish after dish, the fluted pie-crust lifts,
Revealing baked asparagus in cream,
Coffined crusaders, holy in repose,
Dreaming their dream, in green and purple greaves,
Of a stout thrusting at the pagan shrine.
Who would have stomach for such courtesies
As their devout adventuring requires?
I have grown large on cake and other fancies
And the slow pace that goes with their collection,
The paper sack clutched in a singular hand,
The sidewalk shadowed with autumnal hues.

XXIII

To cast aspersions on asparagus
Becomes the mental amorist's lament.
And other table manners: offering
The tilted pinot to an untouched glass
Or violence to an alligator pear,
Tossing a napkin like a sheet aside,
Leaving the table as he leaves a bed
With little done and everything unsaid.
I tried to give up poetry for you.
Sensing you thought that it divided us,
Carved love-seat not quite wide enough for two.

XXIV

The lake I painted bled into the earth.
Its cradle had been spat on by the Witch

And a foul umber stained its ultramarine.
No matter, since I was that vista's hero,
My easel packed, whistling at distances
Beyond the comfortable close-cropped sward.
For what beside my brogues was waveletted
Grew pale at length to an inviting surface.
Which I declined, however, with good grace,
Since lakes are rings, a marriage not a voyage.
You only come upon another shore.

XXV

Your eyes stared at my waistcoat as we danced
Like the beaked nightbird in a jewelled wood.
It was the dance of lawyers, dance of bears,
The ceremonious duty of a feast.
My leather bindings, my Impressionists,
My palace: all in hostage to the dance,
The dance itself in hostage to your beauty.
And yet your beauty faded, and in turn
You gave the wicked Darwish what he asked for,
Thinking it of little value, as he claimed,
New lamps for old, and changed my life for ever.

XXVI

Holly at the piano, gradus ad
Parnassum, Holly with a checking account,
Child of that grandeur off Tehauntepec
Which once returned us to our primal dreams.
Yet folly is to remind us of corruption,
The futile colours of old ecstasies.
Vassals of Vassar, serving out your term
As any whipped novitiate will do,
Remember the prayers to your earthly fathers
And darn your stockings well! The moon will rise
Upon those blues, those pinks, and coffee creams.

XXVII

When gods grow old they settle by their fires
As outcasts do, their buckets glowing with coals,
And starry music turns to honky-tonk.
Through all our separation music has made
Its distillation of the residues,
Urged to its abstractions from my fear
Of losing them, yet still they swarm at will.
They weigh my fingers in a rising tangle
That now hangs like a haunting over me,
A scattering, a drenching, inescapable
As winds of history across the sidewalks.

XXVIII

Would you arrive attendant at that door,
Sleep-wearied, in a fantasy of sounds
That bring you walking into wakefulness?
The chords are puzzles in your uncombed head.
Their intervals narrow your half-closed eyes
To fathom them, for they are bodiless.
You have some memory of being wooed
By such a sound, in such a darkened place,
Where a familiar tramp drips with desire
For shelter, seeing you raise an anxious hand
And turn behind the storm-screen to your dreams.

XXIX

They think you are the wicked Witch from Oz
And I a beast in thrall, in human shape.
Or else you are quite mad, and put away,
And I your keeper. I chase them from the gate
Like little rosy daisies, with a stick.
And always there is your piano, and its bones.
We sleep in distant wings of the flying house,
Heavy with longing for the ordinary.
You are an apparition of my mind,
Locked in the palace of my wilfulness,
Invisible within my poetry.

XXX

The emperor of tawdry treats is still
The emperor of some distinct idea
Which in the being conceived is quite transformed,
As ice and salt are turned, to defy death,
And nothing could be more magnificent.
So I have heard that men at their final breath
Look round them at the strange relations there
And wish for such a coldness on their tongue
That grief might find appropriate celebration
In beggar's food. And yet an emperor
May go a progress through a beggar's guts.

XXXI

An ounce of Cretan bhang is strong enough
To kill an elephant: the Darwish dies!
And yet, of course, the Darwish does not die.
He is the evil one, the Moor, in league
With the eternal Separator of Friends.
Knowing this, we know he'll reappear.
Once in state I held the throne of China
Where crimson eaves were battered by the rain
And the leaves flew wildly. All that I have left
Is that dark place where beauty is recreated,
Brought by the worms into the gate of heaven.

XXXII

Said Hamlet of Polonius to the King:
He is at supper. Not where he eats, but where
He's eaten. This is a prince's poetry.
So much for the company of worms.
And so his play, like any music, plays
Upon the octaves of the living spine
And the hair rises erect, as at a spook
That sways her intermezzo from the grave
To speak mad words or clutch your frozen fingers.
The worm's your only emperor for diet
But poetry's the only heaven we have.

Thun 1947

My mother's evenings: Brahms in Hungarian mood,
Her nails clicking, cigarette ash bombing the keys,
Or feeding the folded hem of a holiday frock
Beneath the pile-driving needle of her Singer
Like a blind woman feeling along a shelf;
Rapt, and to me mysterious, movement of fingers
When notes and stitches stuck and ravelled in lurches
And the face became a mask of intent, like a mirror.

The frock was packed, with its promise of release
From necessary details of dailiness
Like a page from a history of her future life
Torn out to be secretly looked at and admired,
And my father pressed the locks of the fibre suitcase,
Keeping the key safe, with its buff card tag,
And took us off to Europe, on a whim,
As if to inspect it, like a plate, for damage.

The train rattled across recovered France,
Exploring in its ruined library
Cities like classics of a forgotten age.
And my father, younger than my daughters now,
Weary with war and with austerity,
Resolved upon adventure, secure in knowing
The unassailable status of families,
Sacred in all their peculiarities.

His hand rose to his moustache, that moment
Of amusement, self-appraisal, ruminative
Pleasure that would precede a little laugh,
Forefinger smoothing down its surface, the thumb
Concealed, but stroking its base away from the lips,
A flourish that seemed to say: 'Well, here we are!'
Yes, the operation was successful.
Time had smiled on his contrivances.

The suitcase closed in London was opened in
The Bernese Oberland, and if it carried
Its ghostly baggage of separated lives
Across the shores of partings, beyond the past
With its leading questions and tacit promises,
It was not now to say. Our trinity
Was an old romance of sorts, somewhat on show,
Somewhat delayed, yet proving all its worth.

Suddenly I was running across the gravel paths
That were hot to the foot and blinding until dusk.
A close heat settled on the hotel gardens
Where butterflies collapsed upon the borders
And the heavy bee, dragging its dusty pelt,
Grappling and steadying its petal like
A squat wrestler, knew the single thing
That gave its furious purpose to the summer.

Dishes were brought to white tablecloths
By smiling waiters: Kassuppe and dark bread,
Ovals of veal, medallions in their jus,
Yellow and red pears, small Kaffees,
And after dinner the band beneath the trees
Played clumsier and bearlike versions of
The miniature marches and the model polkas
Pricked out by needles in their fretted cases.

Here were my first fireworks, bought to be saved
For days in their coloured paper and thin fuses,
Secretly guarded in quiet wonder for being,
Like books, the labels of all the strange events
That they contained, continually touched,
Till their small narratives burned on the hotel gravel
On the First of August, the Swiss National Day,
Lighting the darkness and the underside of leaves.

And other pleasures: the twenty-centime pieces
Dealt out as in a game and frequently
Replenished, like but unlike sixpences,

Disks of garlands sliding into machines
With an antebellum freedom, a welcoming chlunk
That delivered their boxed portions of *Kaugummi*
With the clatter and swagger of the everyday,
As though this magical life had never stopped.

I was ten, leggy and long before the age
When we are locked into our sex like a punishment.
Every day I walked along the quay
From the Freienhof to the wooden Flussbad's faded
Chocolatey violet, its louvred cubicle half-doors
Clicking and swinging like saloons in westerns,
With the pouches of costumes wrung out and hanging
On rails, smelling of twisted wool and oil.

There I would leap and be swept away in daring
Along the rapid Aare tasting of snow,
A shouting head carried along in the current
And what I shouted lost in the voice-filled air,
Till the soles of my feet settled on sodden wood,
The barrier spanning the width of the rushing river
To keep its bathers from spilling and flowing for ever,
And I was laughing and buoyant, and I could swim.

For the sadness of the seasons and their songs
My star-limbed childhood had no ready ear,
Yet somewhere on the air were all the sounds
That all Thun's summers ever made or heard,
The song itself of song's entitlement
To name the nameless feelings of the heart,
Groth's 'Wie Melodien . . .' which, set by Brahms,
Became his theme for evanescent love:

  'Like melodies, there is this thing
  That haunts but will not stay,
  Like flowers that come in Spring
  And drift like scent away.

  A spoken word begins
  To shape it for my eyes,

When like a mist it thins
And like a breath it dies.

Yet still within each verse
A tender fragrance sleeps,
Coaxed from the bud's tight purse
By an eye that almost weeps.'

It passed me by upon the summer air
As to a wren the purpose of the gods.
It drifted on, beyond the pleasure gardens,
Above the little steamer on the lake
Where couples on the benches at the stern
Half heard its poignant message and reached out
To hold each other as the shoreline passed
And evening settled on the villages.

Now the fireflies rose and fell, in motions
Contrary to any eye which watched them,
And lamps were lit upon the terraces.
The grown-ups talked, sometimes to themselves,
Sometimes to other guests, in dialogue
Whose antiphons, embellished by tobacco,
Evaporated into the still branches
Of lofty trees, gaunt guardians of the night.

There Numa, stumbling after the old lawyer
His master, could bear at last to take the air
Or sit at his laced boots, panting with a grin.
'*Il est malade, tu sais, ce drôle de chien*'
Said our friend. We never knew what the illness was,
Although it was insisted on at length,
So much so that the man himself was known
To us, bearded, pince-nez'd, as 'Malade Chien'.

And Malade Chien gave me when we left
A three-inch wooden bow-legged bulldog
Covered in tan napped cloth, with bright glass eyes
And a painted scowl. It wasn't an ornament.
It wasn't a toy. But a little of the spirit

Of that stocky optimistic doggy life
Which had escaped the rheumy tottering Numa
And his lonely master, seated side by side.

Whatever my father found to say to him
In the weighed deference of conceded language
And the smiles of its imperfect understanding
I never knew, but ran away and played
Upon the baking terraces, like water
That seeks its secret knowledge of gravity,
Spreading itself in a mindless bestowal of favour
Upon the earth which is its safe domain.

Chips of gravel like heavy lumps of sugar,
Feathers, the blood spots of geranium,
Dried larvae, husks: the casual waste of summer,
And a dog's nose reaching down to sniff my play.
Poor Numa, half a century dead and more,
His master, too. My parents twelve years gone,
Though moving briefly in these lines of mine,
Sitting together, piecing out their French.

All that survives of those long days is what
My parents built for me in reaching out
Towards each other, something like an arch,
A space of joy, above me, out of my sight
But in my interest, the inscrutable
Design of their shared, not solitary life
Which an unsearching boy must keep somewhere
Like a toy too old for him, that cost too much.

High on the tilted uplands above the lake,
Just for a moment, I became myself,
Not for the first and not the only time
But at the end of something, and a beginning,
There on a grazed meadow at Goldiwil,
Knowing the distance between the Alps and me
To be no more than a foot-throb from the earth
Beneath me, yet somehow further than the stars.

In some unvisitable yet certainly
Recorded locus of our continuum
I am there still, alive from top to toe:
The lock of hair falling above a grin,
Falling like the long end of my belt,
The cricket shirt, the elbows brown and crooked,
The deep shorts, and the socks reaching to the knees,
The sandals doubly buckled, slightly turned in.

And long I stare at myself without staring back,
For the past, though winding, is a one-way street
And the future unfolds few maps. To be alone
Is a condition of the observing brain,
And something that's remote is better seen,
Like stars or mountains. And the heart goes out
Fiercely if frailly from its uncertain darkness,
Like coloured fires along the terraces.

from SONG & DANCE (2008)

Song of Absence

The space that was filled with the ash tree
Is displaying a desolate blue,
That lack is a path in the bracken
Which led to the ridge with a view,
That gap was a gate that we fastened
To stop ewes and lambs getting through,
And the grass is knee-high in the garden
And the scythe makes a rust of the dew.

The creaking that comes from the stairwell
At the silent tread of a shoe,
The warmth and the crease in a cushion,
The flower in the vase that looks new,
The creosote smell on the gatepost,
The trickling sound from the loo,
The knock on the door that is no one,
The absence upstairs that is you.

The morning has lost its momentum,
The afternoon's nothing to do,
The evening's completely self-centred
And all its assumptions untrue,
But worst is the stillness of night-time,
For ever a quarter-past two
When dwelling on shapes in the darkness
Is no nearer to sleeping, or you.

How Far?

How far is it to Carcassonne?
I'll stir the dust until
I reach that glittering place I crave,
Heat-haunted citadel.

You were away before us,
With something on your mind,
Reckless of all horizon
And all you left behind.

Your friends of the cold morning,
The friends you lived among,
Who worked with you, and fished with you
They heard you sing this song:

'How far is it to Carcassonne?
How difficult to find?
The years run on and on and on
Like waves upon the mind.'

How far is it to Carcassonne?
We sat at night alone.
I knew my heart was full enough.
The sea and shore were one.

You looked away. I heard you say:
'I'm going to Carcassonne.
My weary feet are stoutly shod,
My shoes are full of blood and bone
And while I have my breath, by God,
I'll go to Carcassonne.'

How far is it to Carcassonne?
How difficult to find?
The years run on and on and on
And I am left behind.

Although I do not see an end,
I do not have the patience left
To face blank stares with smiles,
For I shall soon be gone.

The skies are rent, the rock is cleft,
And we shall soon be dead.
How far is it to Carcassonne?
How far is it, how far?

How far is it to Carcassonne?
No trace of you is there,
Nor anywhere upon this road I tread,
Nor anywhere, nor anywhere.

Rascasse

A shoal like a Calder mobile appears
Posing with parallel fins,
Little blue fishes with tails like shears
And well-tuned fears that are better than ears
For sharks with their chinless grins.

And in between the two extremes
Of fry in a state of fright
And the cruising drama of their dreams,
Between the teeth and the prey that teems,
The flight and the terrible bite

Comes a moment of fun, as one by one
There enter the pink rascasse
Wearing a curious look, like a nun
Remembering something private she's done
Halfway through the Mass.

You've seen it in court on the face of Charles Laughton,
That Black Cap, bad-smell leer:
A touch of class like a '99 Corton
Suppressing a snigger like the plays of Joe Orton
Or the mad disgust of *Lear*.

On a fish of a certain size, you know,
Self-righteousness sits oddly,
But the surliness is only for show:
Their thoughts as they twiddle to and fro
Are plaintive and ungodly.

(The sea's an old bowl of soup, my dears,
And we are the tipsy frosh.
It's been about for a billion years
And it's salty like the sting in tears
That doesn't come out in the wash.

A crusty fish, a whiskered fish,
Must never, but never, lose face.
The song expresses our fervent wish
Not to end up in a steaming dish
With the rest of the bouillabaisse.)

CHORIC SONG

'The hand that placed the planets loosed the thunder.
The hand that piped the blood betrayed a blunder.
The hand that made the blunder sent a flood.
The hand that formed the flounder gave it mud.
    Rascasse! Rascasse!
    A rose sedan! A mailed cuirass!
    Marine retread of Zinedine Zidane!
    Late call? Doubtful ball!
Anything's better than ending up dead.

The hand that fingered Adam was the same.
The hand that bluffed the baize gave up the game.
The hand that raised the city made a bid.
The hand that stirred the squirlu squashed the squid.
    Rascasse! Rascasse!
    Enversez-moi une demi-tasse!
    Just like I said (mwah! mwah!)
    Vents violents? Soyez prudents!
Anything's better than ending up dead.

The hand that rocked the cradle rocked the rocks.
The hand that signed the paper felled the ox.
The hand that calmed the waters lit the hob.
The hand that made the soup turned up the knob.
    Rascasse! Rascasse!
    Godfrey Daniel! Godfrey Cass!
    King Charles's head! King Charles's spaniel!
    Rouille? Phooey!
Anything's better than ending up dead.'

My Life on the Margins of Celebrity

I sat on Beatrix Lehmann's knee, terrified that she was undead;

I saw Laurel and Hardy alive at the Lewisham Hippodrome, and they were gratified by my laughter;

I bowed to Queen Mary, widow of George V, in Greenwich Park, and from her limousine of midnight hue she nodded graciously back;

I was inspected in full uniform by Field-Marshal Montgomery: his cornflower-blue eyes passed within twenty inches of mine, and he departed in a bullet-proof car;

I sang for Vaughan Williams, his great head sunk on his waistcoat, neither awake nor asleep;

I watched Jonathan Miller lift a white mouse by its tail and drop it in a killing-bottle for me as an illustration of something or other;

I saw Frank Swift pick up a football with one hand;

I waited in the wings for my own entrance while Oliver Sacks played de Falla's 'Ritual Fire Dance' in a sash and a lurid spotlight;

I asked T. S. Eliot what he was writing, and his answer shall remain a secret;

I rang up the curtain on Dennis Potter in his first public performance, playing the part of a Romanian-French playwright;

I trod the throbbing boards of an ocean liner with Burt Lancaster, who was very small, and who smiled his characteristically delicate sneering smile;

I was asked to stay on in my first job, but politely declined and was succeeded in office by the Earl of Gowrie;

I drove Edward Albee to Niagara Falls, where he was silent among the thickly-iced trees;

I held Sam Mendes in my arms, but was more interested
in his father's collection of Japanese pornography;

I brushed away cobwebs that had been sprayed on my hair
by David Attenborough;

I played heads-bodies-and-legs with Henry Moore;

The Poet Laureate sent me reams of his verse, which I
regretfully refused to publish;

I handed Debra Winger a glass of wine and did not tell her
who I was;

I played against William Golding's French Defence and
infiltrated my King's Knight to d6 and he couldn't
avoid going a piece down;

And all this is true, and life is but a trail of dust between
the stars;

The unremembered shall be forgotten, and the remembered
also;

The dead shall be dead, and also the living.

Variation on Shapcott

When the Old Man suddenly rubbed me awake
I was already aroused, yawning and reaching upwards,
Skinny as a rib, just a slip of a something
With a taut belly and extremely long legs.
I knew immediately what I was intended for,
Dropped like a hairy yet naked egg
Into such a heavily populated garden.
But that gracile creature with his delicate yard
Lolling like a pink comma across his leg
Was not the greatest thing I was up against.
When the Old Man nudged me into his arms
I could only think: nothing will come of nothing
With all that other wild howling pulling me downwards,
Proboscis, slung bull, ape-gland, snake.

The Poet Orders his Marriage at
St Marylebone Church

RB and EBMB, 12 September 1846

1

In and out I weave
Like a double double u
And the pillars patient as spindles receive the waiting skein.
In and out, and back
And forth, I await my cue
Where Hardwick's Corinthian nods to Nash's *mise-en-scène*.

2

Outside, the daily hubbub,
The ordinary rush
Of flies, with the spin and bounce of their wheels as they speed to the city.
Inside, the timeless silence,
A whiff of the old God-hush
That induces a wonder at infinite pain and infinite pity.

3

Six pillars, six
Minutes (I counted them off)
That it takes at her pace of quavers to get to the steps of the church:
From her father's ignorance
To the beadle's inquisitive cough
Full six unending minutes, I found in my fond research.

4

With the licence in my pocket
I made my own rehearsal,
Counted the steps and minutes that will seal the loving decision
Which now is set on its course,
Running without reversal
To the full and final chords of its grand initial vision.

With the licence in my pocket
And my inmost self professing
A ready trust in the service of the heart to be born afresh,
    I demanded the plainest rites:
    The text that defines God's blessing,
The touch of his finger that feels for the soul and makes one flesh.

    The sexton under the tower
    With his ready foot in a stirrup
Offered to tread the bells, but I said I would have no bells.
    The organ's *unda maris*
    Was oozing out like syrup,
But I forbade it: nothing but Goldhawk's book of spells.

    Now six minutes since
    She left her house for me
And here I wait with my loving cousin declaring his fitness
    To sign me over to life
    And love eternal, and she
With a steady tread to meet me here, and her maid as witness.

    We are love's actors, we
    Are waiting in our wings,
Watched by the critical world and gilded angels' faces
    Smudged with the smoke of theatre,
    Where the psalmist surely sings
That our lines are fallen unto us in pleasant places.

9

She who has been invited
Will shortly be in sight,
And the tide is running like dreams before the light of the morning.
The blood says, This is your chance
To get there by candlelight,
And life draws its bearded and dripping anchor without warning.

10

Unload me at hot Cythera
With the harbourmaster's winch
And let my barrels be broached by love inspecting her borders!
Uncork my animal spirits
And pour out half an inch
And let the attentive future stand by awaiting my orders!

11

What shall they be? To be drained
To the last drop, to aspire?
Or to add one thing to another, the daily considered choice?
To lie in the swoon of the spirit
Or to spark and to take fire
Till the body survives its sentence and becomes a sounding voice?

12

Our wish, as we know, is both
The sum of its small attentions
And the large idea which has no distinct embodiment,
Until we suddenly find it
Declaring its intentions
And making its claim upon us, as being what we meant.

13

And so by indirection
We move towards a goal
That is always revealed to us in stages, like a play:
We try to learn our parts
And the parts are parts of a whole
That we must write ourselves, yet act out straight away.

14

The future bows politely:
It will surely do our will
As much as time can spare and decency allows,
And though it disapprove
It takes its wages still
And looks on silently with amused and lifted brows.

15

As for the sullen past,
It is left with nothing to do
But to squirrel away its secrets under rusty locks
Or feign forgetfulness
Or suddenly turn on you
And become your guilty familiar, an insistent chatterbox.

16

Only the moment is pure
Of connivance and accusation.
Only the moment itself is free of the hope or regret
That soon enough crowds upon
Our glad improvisation.
Only the moment has not yet learned to fear or forget.

17

Now it is time to act
As the four of us meet together,
And little is said as hands touch, heads incline and smile
In rueful acknowledgement that
It is insignificant whether
We walk in inappropriate pairs or in bridal style.

18

But like a dawn duel,
Each plighted and their second
Enters bravely through the mists of their unwished furtiveness.
None to give, or be given?
No one till now has reckoned
On the power of old tradition over bold assertiveness.

19

For a faint failing of form
Haunts the thing we want
To proceed without procedure (as though such a thing could be),
Makes us wince at the beadle's collar,
The verger's hat in the font,
The uncleared coils of rope, and such incongruity.

20

And now, as the words are recited
And we suddenly reach the most
Significant part of the play, the ring in the hot clasped glove,
There is a ghost here.
It is your father's ghost,
The living, the absent, the terrible – terrible in his love.

21

He stands where he ought to stand,
Unseen, unknowing, unknown,
And I feel him growing there like a frigid chill in the blood,
Like Acrisius in his tower,
Like Mozart's statue of stone,
Like the dragon defending the apples of gold, like a worm in the bud.

22

And his ghost eyes the yellow ring
Placed on the leather book,
The blind-tooled commonplace blue of a Book of Common Prayer,
As the curate takes it up
With hardly so much as a look
And gives it back to me for you and your finger to wear.

23

And just for a moment I quail
Before the invisible glare
That lingers with disbelief, and will continue to linger
Upon that empty shape
Resting on God's word there,
Heavy with our intent, now full upon your finger.

24

But dearest, our ghosts we defy:
In a moment the thing is done,
As a boat whose pilot sees her out through the widening estuary
Is at once in the open sea,
And we together are one
With the strangely familiar shape of our names in the dust of the vestry.

25

You pause as if in a dream
And are given a glass of water,
And you start again in these first few minutes of married life
To sign, in unbelief
That you are still a daughter
(Or so you must name yourself) before you may be a wife.

26

And the talkative, puzzled verger,
Happy to take my gold,
Attempts on the steps to assert the sanctity of marriage
To a couple apparently reckless,
Though clearly disturbingly old,
Who leave him in rapt mid-sentence, each to their separate carriage.

27

And those six pillars support
A triumphant cupola
As a working week lays abundant groundwork for our devotion,
And high above our journey
There shines a single star
Compelling our hearts like keels to the receiving ocean.

28

The church itself is unchanged,
Yet silently proclaims
From its hallowed space, as it reaches aloft from London's grime,
That here have been safely lodged
An eager pair of names
That will lie in the annals of the parish, and of time.

The Captain's Galop

Quickly running sideways: such an idiotic thing to do,
Arms around the waists of sexual persons either side of you!

Portholes show the ocean lifting: when the deck begins to tilt
Dancing feet continue to express a faith in how it's built.

Locked together, silk to flannel, epaulette to mutton-sleeve,
Men and women not related boldly pair and interweave.

Hugged so closely, don't you feel the secret grinding of the hips,
Like a millipede proceeding drunkenly with little skips?

Might you care to flick an ankle? Squeeze a bottom? Laugh out loud?
Once the fiddlers start to sweat you'll find that little's disallowed.

Chin up high, and beaming, face the left as you approach the right,
Smartly turn the head to starboard, giving whoops of pure delight.

Always looking back to where you came from when you make the turn,
Measuring each distance with a merry air of unconcern.

Underneath you, ocean turning restlessly from side to side,
Salt illimitable litres mindlessly preoccupied.

Captain's table: dizzy still, the dancers turn to langoustines.
Silver ladles swirl like hands of clocks around the soup tureens.

Baudroie, merlan, grondin, vive, goggle up from bouillabaisse,
Challenging Lord Challenger to look them calmly in the face.

Mrs Thing attempts a pudding (ewe's cheese, sugar, eau-de-vie).
Angela's left knee beneath the table feels another knee.

Fruit and walnuts, laughs and murmurs, sweet phlogiston of cigars.
Captain's toast: the poised ecstatic metaphysics of the stars.

North to south and east to west unbroken line of night and sea,
Scattered in their milky dome the lights in vague immensity.

Named once for the legions of the heavens supervising earth,
Minting men and women with their life-long character at birth.

Glasses raised, the stars are praised in sips of port for all they teach,
Light fingers of applause, the tug of chairs, and now the Captain's speech:

'Whither bound, and why? The thumping questions tease as questions will,
Searching in the testaments for some revealing codicil.

God made everything there is, from cochineal to caribou.
God who made the boundless waters turned his hand to me and you.

Apemen, alemen, archers, abbots, applewomen, advocates,
Educators, engineers, eccentrics, excommunicates,

Introverts, inspectors, intellectuals, irrationalists,
Owners, overseers, officials, oboists, oenologists,

Unbelievers, utter bastards, underlings, utopians:
Each vocation has its blueprint somewhere in his doodled plans.

Ask me how I know this? I'm the Captain. I must know.
Pilot, vicar, host, philosopher and impresario.

Souls entrusted to my care and *nothing* ever left to chance,
Daily orders, perfect freedom, all you have to do is dance.

Don't you bless me for your pleasures? Don't you leap at my commands?
Know your destiny is safely locked away and in my hands?

Dance the dance in every calm and dance the dance through every storm.
Dance the headlong dance that dancing surely meant us to perform.

Keep the dancing line unbroken, dance together, never stop.
Dance the Captain's dance. The bouncing, hectic, thunderous Galop!'

The Figue Maxixe

Green outside and pink within,
Figs must be the fruit of sin.
Le long de l'esplanade de Nice
Suck them and dance the Figue Maxixe:
Wearing a great big sticky grin,
D'abord on tord, et puis on glisse.
That's how to do the Max, Max,
That's how to do the Figue Maxixe.

Princesse de Polignac est protectrice,
Protège de génie et Des Six.
Elle donne le sein à son salon,
Et ô ses petits mamelons
Américains! They make you shiver.
So does the down upon her Swanee River.
That's where they learned the Max, Max,
That's where they learned the Figue Maxixe.

Elle est si raffinée. Elle est exquise.
Elle port les pyjama en raies cerises.
Princess of the sewing machine,
Elle donne de l'argent et de sa poitrine.
First one foot and then the other:
Who's the baby? Who's the mother?
She dotes upon the Max, Max,
Si raffolée du Figue Maxixe.

The Princess wears a cakewalk wig.
The Princess just adores a fig,
Petit sac avec semence:
Dans son douceur elle s'y enfonce.
Ses lèvres lestes se reconnaissent:
D'abord elles tordent et puis elles glissent
That's how she does the Max, Max,
That's how she does the Figue Maxixe.

Princesse de Polignac est très polie.
Princesse de Polignac n'est point poilue.
L'enfer blanc du Piz Palu
A fait son maquillage pâli.
Princess de Polignac est ma délice,
And most of all I like her knees,
So let's all do the Max, Max,
Let's all do the Figue Maxixe.

The Orbital Samba

The lights on the shore and the crowds as they roar and
    the rhythm are leading you townwards
And the drums as they beat get into your feet like the rum
    when the bottle tilts downwards
And it runs through the veins where it plans its campaigns
    like Wellesley before Salamanca.
Your arms are in bud with splayed fingers and blood; each
    side-kick you give is a spanker.
One hip like a rocket departs from its socket while the other
    revolves on its axis
And the whole body sways as the pelvis sashays and the
    spine absolutely relaxes.
You decide that it's pleasant to feel deliquescent and notice
    that people around you
With their arms in the air and with glittering hair are edging
    their way to surround you,
For you are the star that they sense from afar like matter
    obedient to gravity,
The luminous centre they all wish to enter, the focus of
    total depravity.
Your limbs are balletic, your skin is magnetic, your gaze is
    compelling as granite,
Your merest inaction's a fatal attraction, the force that sets
    spinning the planet.
No wonder the dance is biology's chance to shuffle its cards
    for the future:
Not only the samba but also the mambo, the maypole, the
    Minnie-the-Moocher,
The Palais at Harlesden, the can-can, the Charleston, the
    knees-up, the Countess of Cavan,
The one-in-a-million, the twist, the cotillion, the polka, the
    brawl and the pavane,
The Highlander's sword-dance, the fling, the Gay Gordons,
    the Iroquois war-dance, the goose-step,
The Argentine tango, the reel, the fandango, the clog-dance,
    the one-step, the two-step.

You're surrounded by persons whose self-control worsens
as their hair falls to pieces when the tempo increases
(in the greeny-brown light it's Pre-Raphaelite, all
bouncing and frizzy: think Rossetti and Lizzy) and you
can't get away from the flashing array of criss-crossing
lasers and stoned star-gazers; the infant heart-breakers
and quivering Quakers and ecstasy-fakers; the mischief-
makers, tattooed undertakers and lewd Sabbath-
breakers; the amateur Shakers and Josephine Bakers:
it's enough to send you bananas.

The Quaquaversal Jig

Left, right, feeling your own sides,
Smoothing down the waist.
     Your hips jut
As you level the ground about you
     With concentration.
     Left. Right.
Such pow-wow tells the body
It has become the god it worships.
     Your eyes are shut
     In self-admiration.

Left, right, brushing the cobwebs away,
Peering through the weight of the music.
     A duck and a hunch,
Cocking the head on the shoulders,
     Stomping on the spot.
     Left. Right.
Such sense of body needs no witness,
No agreement to touch, no devotion.
     Thanks a lot.
     Thanks a bunch.

from PEBBLE & I (2010)

Fragment of a Victorian Dialogue

I asked her: 'Since it is easy to imagine
The unimaginable illnesses
(The bones of the fingers turning into jelly,
Hairs growing in the socket of an eye)
Why is it that we never comprehend
The incomprehensible ones?' She smiled,
Stroking Pebble, her favourite, for its long
Descent into itself and for its utter
Complicity in such a passive process,
Feeling nothing and expecting nothing.
'Because you look for reasons (came the reply)
Of malice, or revenge upon misuse.
Expecting giant rebukes (the confiscation
Of an outraged organ or the disintegration
Of the disputed systems), you do not see
That all is accidental, the result
Of overreaching experiment, of pure
Incompetence. For failure is not a judgement,
It is systemic: the eventual restoration
Of the somatic miracle to common
Matter.' But I, not knowing whether to think
Any matter either common or uncommon,
Given the sport of things existing at all,
Turned to her pale sister who most affected
Me and my kind, feelingly, at the end:
'Why (this was my question) is the event,
The irreversible and final decline,
Accompanied by your severe attention,
Not merely warning, since warnings now were useless,
But painting the withdrawal of your sister
In the cruel colours of a felt collapse?'
And the sister did not smile, but half turned
Away, as if in genuine disappointment.
'Do you not know (she said) that all your pleasure,
All your pain, are all the same, and mine?
They are my gift, in infinite shades within
The body's deep sensorium. Without me

There would be nothing to tell you you exist,
And what I give I cannot take away.'
And so the supreme sisters hand in hand
Went from that place, each with their plaything,
The blithe elder with Pebble, the troubled younger
With the unwilling object of her own
Makeshift, hurtful and unstinting love.
I was not Pebble, and did not want to be.

Seven Vials

She gave me seven vials
Ranked in their colours, bright
As old flags once were.

The first had a dull glow,
Pale as the earliest flowers:
It weighed like a stone in my hand.

The second, a living green,
Seemed to have nowhere to go
But stirred like a leaf in my hand.

The third held a commonplace
Azure of emptiness
And died like hope in my hand.

The fourth was a ripe fruit
Trapped in its purple glass:
It stayed like a bruise on my hand.

The fifth with its stink of death
Laboured to shed its rust
And clung like ice to my hand.

The sixth contained embers
Of a vital distillation
And pulsed like a vein in my hand.

The seventh was the indigo
Of pure questioning
And moved like a hand in my hand.

These were to be poured
In order, and in order
To be for a time preserved.

Spilling and sometimes mixing,
Elements of the eternal
In the ceremony of life.

Yao Defen

As I duck my head beneath a playhouse door
I feel myself at once in my grandmother's house
Where I used to think I might be small for ever
And people would lift the heavy tasselled cloth
To peer at me, playing beneath a table,
And smile that unguarded smile of pretended surprise.

Generally we are the size we like to be,
And for a time we are perfectly content
To know more about the underside of drawers
Than bother about the things that are kept inside them,
To listen from little cupboards without real interest
And to squeeze among the lost trophies of attics.

Then to arrive at last at our proper elevation
And to inherit the true scale of our being
Is to find that the world treats us on the level.
No one looks down on us, and hardly up.
There is almost nothing that we are not equal to.
Our height is our relief at being ordinary.

But what do we make of the beautiful poet who
At four-foot six is not the rake he feels?
Or this solemnity on her fortified chair
Who at seven-foot eight is the tallest woman in Asia?
Their lives are miraculous adventures, where
They reach in longing for all that is beyond them.

Ah, but we are all locked into some sadness,
Strangers to our bodies, victims of
Our radiant but unattended smile,
Our welcoming but suffocating embrace,
And their surrender at last in rooms already booked
For them, gratis, at the Hotel Necropole.

Small Room in a Hotel

In this cool cube of marble
I am valid but invisible
As an image caught in a camera
But not yet reproduced.

My reappearance from confinement
Is that of a lavatory Houdini
Except that no one notices
And the wonder is reduced to a trickle.

How many men have died at stool,
Bent in that vain rictus of hope
That gives to their flushed features
The terrifying squint of a Samurai?

Between philosophical reflections
And the final rebellion of blood
Is the same fine line as between shadows
And the ignorant earth which casts them.

Why are we so eager for shadows?
Is reality so hard to bear?
That our root is in earth which
Returns to earth, and is our sleep?

Each day, wherever we are,
We should rehearse this cancelled debt,
Like a sacrifice whose incense
Ascends into the purity of thought.

Anecdote of an Amphibious Amateur

A man is standing on a wave.
His hands appear to be conducting
An invisible orchestra.

The wave is hollowed out in
The colour of old ink bottles.
Tons of it hang in the air.

But time is only at rehearsal.
Faltering, it picks up its pace
And the wave is delivered to the shore.

Where, to the tearing sound of applause,
Its completed chords collapse
Into a dispersal of boiling snow.

And the man? Once nobly erect,
Now folded under, he knows
That the music is larger than he is.

The Love Thread

Two little love birds fly in and out
Of the arching sarsaparilla hedge,
Neither greeting nor ignoring the other.
This is what they do, no notion
Of self-performance, no sense of habit.
For them, purpose lies in the doing:
The breasting of the wind, the falling back,
The spooling of an invisible thread
Of fluttering and separation
Before they cross again, like a tied
Bow, over and over and over.
This is their annual wooing in the blue
Above the trowel-leaves of the hedge,
And in the hedge, where life breeds.
But now they have nested in a basket
Hanging above the shed for old shoes
And lobster-pots, as if chancing
A brave familiarity
With the nude lords of their demesne,
Though Ange says they have abandoned it
Now that the summer makes things busy.
So there is nothing more to say.

The Pagoda Revisited

Chanteloup, Amboise

This monument to a view of nothing
(Its abolished château) has every reason
To admire itself for its persistence.
At the end of a peaceable gravel drive
Among well-watered swans, its tiers
Provide a circular ascent in stages
Like the ages of man. But here we are at the
Top suddenly, aware of the crumbling stone
And iron reinforcement of the loose rails.
It is as narrow as being in your own head,
And you can think of nothing but getting down.

Card Houses

The air was angry all the night,
Drum-rolling on the dormer
And bottle-blowing the chimney.

I thought maybe that the mountain
Was taking revenge on the roof
For the stealing of slate.

The day that the deck was dealt
Out to the village, violence
Was proposed to its profile.

The scope of the sky was altered.
Stone was split and stacked,
Transported, and nailed to timbers.

Houses deserve to be dry,
But a hill needs a level head
Not to quarrel with a quarry.

The wind is a reminder of wrath,
A momentary mineral alliance,
The dunning of a debt.

Its fingers grip the gutters,
Twisting and tugging at the eaves.
The roof comes loose like a lid.

And vaults all over the valley,
Slates flapping their feathers,
Blue-black as ravens.

Slates stream like a causeway,
A conjuror's spurted shuffle
Frittering over the fields.

So I thought, deep in our duvet,
Listening to the lost leaves
And the thrashing of the ash tree.

But it was only my heart's hammering
And fear of the frailness of houses,
Only my silly sleeplessness

That spoke to me of spooks
And warned of walls and windows
Left standing in shapes of stone

Trembling to tumble inwards
At the barest of breaths,
One after the other.

In the shadowing sun of the morning
The mountain was itself once more,
Looking calm enough in its keep.

It wore the appearance of apex
In that vague violet of a grey
That has endured epochs.

And there was no hint of harm:
Songbirds settling on the slates
Reckoned them as good as rock

And the angles argued respect
For their share of local shape
In every particular point.

Since the world hosts our happiness
It is only proper to presume
That there is mountain enough for men.

It has endured erosion,
And appears altogether
Calm about collapsing.

In any case, we conclude
That the future will have forgotten
Our naturally tumbling towers

And what we dare in our depredations
Is nothing like the nemesis
That time idly toys with.

Platform

The stillness of this mountain halt,
Rails curving in the sun around
The bend into a dark wood,
Is like surprising in oneself
An insight into the possible.

To walk up here, to find by chance
A steel intention palpable
Among these ancient oaks, with slate
And rhododendrons collapsed and sprawling,
Is to stumble upon a wonder.

The wooden platform is no more
Than a stand to raise you from the nettles
And filleted bones of fern that crowd it.
You might stare in each direction for hours
And at your wristwatch with impatience.

To deliver speeches while you wait
Would be a natural consequence
Of the mild and philosophical
Excitement in which you find yourself,
But there is no one who would hear you.

Except the inconsequential birds
Shitting berries in a clearing,
Who call only to each other
And listen only for like sounds
That have some likely meaning for them.

It is a museum of lost journeys,
The suspended survival of a decision
To join two useful distances
By the latest means. At either end
The purpose has been long forgotten.

Your footsteps lightly creak upon
This pulpit of the afternoon.
The moment is one of all too few
Within the strange parentheses
Of your own origin and end.

Koshka

1

Sometimes you came to ask a question:
That silent arresting look of yours,
A lift of the head, the kneading of paws,
   The slowest of slow blinks
And a pretence of unconcern.
   You will not ask it now.

Empty, the places where you sat:
The window's vantage, or the edge
Of wall, or disregarded ledge
   Where you could face your foes,
A yellow carpet patch of sun.
   You will not sit there now.

Your movements noticed here and there,
Your steady ruminating walk
From room to room, that ambling stalk
   As if in quest of something
Partly assembled in your mind.
   You will not go there now.

Your eyes were the liquid mirrors of distance
When all the things we couldn't see
Became for you the two or three
   Significant images
That gave your leaping body purpose.
   You will not see them now.

In age, your head would sometimes droop
When sitting quietly in a doze,
And lift again, as if the nose
   Took up its sentry post,
Prompted by some delicious dream.
   You will not lift it now.

2

Where you are is the nowhere that we fear,
The spaceless unappetising future, the past
Before memory, the present without being.
You did not know it was about to happen,
Lost in my cradling arm, the lightness of a doll
Whose head, empty of life, dropped back.

That was our knowledge, ours the final vigil
Once the fatal arrangements had been made.
The knowledge is our pain, also our gift
That lets me write these lines in celebration
Of a small blue cat, nervous of disposition
But friendly and attentive when so inclined.

It is an unwelcome gift, hateful to think it.
Knowing how soon the secret sluices of the body
Rust in their ratchets, how the glistening glands
Dry to a throb of stone and pause in their pulse,
Is to know a truth as fixed as a date on a coin
Thoughtlessly hoarded, that is still to spend.

For it is our death that we somehow mourn
In yours, still pacing the enchanting towers
And terraces where we must waste our days,
And this is our own life to be spilled out through
Our hooped reluctant arms, as though releasing
A cat aching and eager to be away.

Piano Masterclass

For Rolf Hind

1

The piano is opened
And lifts a hopeful wing.

Phrases are to be freed
From their locked pace

From the weather of flat fingers
And the impositions of posture.

Scriabin unscrambled
From code to cadence

From half-vision
To the visionary.

2

It sits forward on its knuckles
Glossy as a gorilla.

Its bared teeth
Are neither a smile nor a snarl.

Beneath its raised eyebrows
A swarm of mixed signals

Which must be confronted
With a patient stroking.

Its great roaring
Is an eventual liberation.

3

The feckless prelude,
The necklace unpearled

And now to be restrung,
The picture rehung

The proportions restored
And the fingers grateful

For their sudden release
And disappearance up the ladder

Like a cloud of peace,
Like a flight of angels.

4

Debussy's poorly piano
Is making good progress.

Delicate exercises,
Pressing and pointing.

The first cautious steps
Of a spacious dance.

The renewed stamina,
The unlooked-for elation.

The plurality of notes,
The singularity of idea.

5

Brahms in slow-motion,
All arms and fists.

The thunder is broken
Into clumsy pieces

Peering into the notes
As into a middle distance

Or the eye of a storm
That will whirl us away

One day, one day,
The hands perfectly full.

Shells

Sun brings out the dazzle on this
Glittering stretch of lonely beach.
Treading on the sizeable sand
You find that its dry creaking bulk
Is a bright random assemblage
Of large grains and very small shells,
Each of the latter the dead hulk
Of some lost watery comma,
A once-determined sea-creature
Who for a paltry length of time
Added its voice to the sea's rage.

In your hand they tell of marvels
Performed on these warm granite coasts:
The orange-and-tan fan smaller
Than a child's little fingernail,
The teardrop whelk, the snail's spiral
Green like a tennis eyeshade and
Hardly bigger than a match head.
This display turns us into gods
Proceeding to our vain pleasures
Across billions of jewels
That were sea-houses, and their ghosts.

The Jetsam Garden

For Felix

On a reach of sun-baked pebbles near the tide-line
Where the stumbling beach lifts slightly like the fine
Barely-shifting gradient of a recumbent body,
Lodged in that untrudged no-man's-land between
The groin of the swirling rocks and the tousled headland

The garden is still visible in its surprising extent
As an unusual enclave of perpendicular shapes,
Like a city seen from a jet on its final descent
Or a placement of toys left out on a carpet
Whose pattern itself had prompted their arrangement.

Blind eyes staring from their igneous mass,
The pebbles wear only the chalky shadow
Of the colours that the sea drenches them in
As it picks them up and slowly turns them
Over in the season of its distress, like problems.

They nudge now in little mounds and lines,
And stuck among them are the dried sprays of fir,
Straws, twigs and plastic ice-cream spines
(White, cerise, magenta, vermilion)
That constitute the garden's vegetation.

Some stones serve as pedestals in places
For fragile figures in their avenues:
Sea urchins, salt-whitened screw-caps, driftweed,
Aquiline half-pegs with blue string arms, surround
The heroes of extemporised civic spaces.

A half-inch cowboy hat in silent cheers
Twirls on a leaning tower of split bamboo.
Another flies a fan of feathers bound
With greenish wire, crusty and oxidised,
Above a mosaic face, cork nose, shell ears.

And charcoal legends elevated there
Look on benignly at the plinths and towers.
There are proprietary names, and a sign
That points in the one direction that it would
Ever occur to it to point: 'La Mer'.

You appraised it, as an architect might do,
With the lordly detachment of a limpet monocle.
You returned with the helpful delivery of new
And unlikely materials ('Here we go!')
And the patient splitting and twiddling of their parts.

And now a week has passed, and you are gone.
The garden hears nothing but the tranquil sea.
Absence is not only a necessary absenting,
When we imagine an elsewhere entered upon
Like a new chapter in an exciting story.

It is also, and much more, a palpable ache
That refuses every hope and compensation.
It is the loneliness of the places that we make,
Like the little garden without you, lost in itself
And in the blankness of nothing to do, or to be done.

Libeccio

The orange petals lift in the libeccio
Like the shoulders of girls being kissed upon the neck.
It shifts the random spillage along the terrace
(Breadcrumbs, grape-pips, toenails, pistachio-shells)
Like a gambler counting his chips to the table edge
And letting them drop into a practised palm.
It blows across the rapt profile of siesta,
Legs tucked up on the day-bed, the hand on the cheek,
And the mind exploring in wonder its gift from the bottle.
The hanging strips of the terrace curtain stir,
Cream/chocolate/amber/chocolate/cream,
With a distant whisper of insistent gossip,
And the sea begins to tear itself to pieces.

We have shut ourselves from these continuous sounds
As having no urgent claim on our peaceful dreams.
But perhaps we should take note of its querulous meddling,
This warm wind whose ambition is to be spent
Here and now at our centre of consciousness.
It blows with a sense of its belated longing,
Like an old man in the sudden fullness of memory,
Salacious, wistful, destructive, impotent.

Paestum

For Peter Porter at eighty

Yesterday the sinuous Amalfi coast,
With its netted lemons the size of babies' heads;
Today a bleaker stretch towards the south,
An outpost of eleventh-century Byzantium
Where a poet's hunger for eternity
Can be fairly matched by the philosopher's
Nostalgia for the accidence of birth.
The place was named for Poseidon, shape-changer,
Greedy for the bodies of boys, and is the site
Of fluted temples devoted to appeasement
Of the sea's fury and its impermanence.
We could both, couldn't we, easily visualise
That English poet who idly wandered here
In his ambition and his amorous exile?

On seeded ruins licked by scuttling lizards
(Who for a moment pause, their pale blue throats
Pulsing with life beneath their chequered green
And black) he himself in his lizardly pleasure
Paused, waistcoat unbuttoned to the sun,
To admire the mountains through the open roof
Of Neptune's temple, broken to the clouds.
At such a moment, verse is one response
To earnest glimpses of the infinite,
And ignorance the best excuse of youth.
The sea would have him soon, yawning over
His jaunty yacht, plucking with sated relish
The sodden legs, and hair, and the clutched hat,
The mountains declining his Promethean myth.

But the philosopher, for whom a glass among friends
Was the right response to an intuition of death
And who embraced it willingly in his high
Symbolic dive into that element
Which is for ever and ever changing shape,
Had long ago made his loving farewells
To talk, companionship, the search for truth;
Long ago had settled his account
With the irrelevant temples and all the little
Uncompleted tasks that filled his day;
Long ago had said good-bye to longing,
And to the sun, and to the lizard-shadowed stone,
Tucked in his head, and put his hands together
In the gesture that is both prow and prayer – and plunged.

The Tongue and The Heart

A pretty little space between the Tongue & the heart,
like that between East & West.
                    Coleridge, *Notebooks*, May 1799

1 Hemispheres

As with the hemispheres,
So between the ears
There is a space we seek
And that is where we speak.

This is what we say.
This is what we feel.
There is a space between,
And that is what we mean.

Love has no East or West,
And surely love knows best
How between tongue and heart
Words must play their part.

And yet this is not all:
Two hemispheres recall
The world where they belong,
The world that is their song.

2 Sunset

Come and look at the sun!
Look at the flagging sun:
Tired of the day he made,
A perfect arch of a day.
He is wrapping it up in the sky
And saving it up for tomorrow.
In these hours of the evening
He thinks he can do better.

A careless teacher, the sun,
Although we dearly love him:
So many days he wastes,
Gathering all the pieces,
Or throwing them away,
Frustrated or in tears.
In these days of our evening
We know we can do better.

3 Pichet

A little jug of wine
    And glasses for two:
Yours, of course, and mine.
    Just for me and you.

Glazed breakable clay
    And full to the spout
On the exciting day
    When we shared it out.

The wine went overboard
    At every tilt
Of the jug we so eagerly poured,
    Reckless of whether it spilled.

Whenever we lifted the jug
    We could not decide
How much of its weight and glug
    There might be left inside.

Though all that we've attempted
    Has come to pass
And the jug nearly emptied,
    There's still wine in the glass.

4 Lizard

He was here before us
And this is his stone.
In the day-long sunshine
Shadow is his home.

His small flanks are dappled
With the ready-made
And myriad concealments
Of light and shade.

Little lick of a tail,
A scamper in the dust,
And no way of counting
The hours as they pass.

We are old sweethearts
With playful language
And fond silence
For camouflage.

Together we take note of
The lizard's calligraphy
Upon his finished stone:
It's his eternity.

5 Headlands

Near you always, just a step behind you
   As the headland rises before us
      And the hills tumble to the sea.

And should there be one more after this one
   You will want to walk there for the view.
      And if you, then surely me.

On they extend, as the coast curves ahead:
　A different view of something
　　That for a moment has no name.

Look behind you: the distance we've travelled
　Seems too great for the time we've taken.
　　For what's to come it is much the same.

6 Puzzle

Within my arms there is a space
That aches for you, though you are there
Just over the horizon
Of the passing moment,
Reading a book, or in a chair.

Heads together under the water,
Heads together over sky,
Patient until its edges
Form their promise of
A landscape of the by-and-by.

There is a story in all shape.
There is memory in an embrace.
And things like missing pieces
Eventually turn up
Like love, in their hiding place.

7 Crossing

The throbbing deck still warm
To the cautious soles of the feet,
Heads touching at the prow,
Music settled to its beat.

Though the wake may be troubled,
Our course is a smooth curve.
In the still velvet of the air
The vessel holds its nerve.

Onward, steadily,
Onward under the stars!
Fire streaks from the zenith,
Night unlocks her armoires!

Pomme

Although the sea, with its senseless political grievance,
Has resumed its recent attempts upon the shore
And a shrapnel of spray falls back upon the rocks
In a careless sluicing, the surface is not unfriendly.
Your flip-flops in the crevice, your launching foot-splash,
The squat breathing-tube, the swell of the maillot,
Reveal that you are still undaunted by the waves.
Behind the glass of your aquarium headpiece
The underseascape is a framed display,
A locked stare, as from a *dix-huitième*
Scaphandre, at an unfamiliar salon
Whose hosts are welcoming, though a trifle insolent.

Here is a slow bogue making cow-eyes, and
Suddenly changing direction like a dodgem.
Boops boops! The alarm is not absolute,
Just nature's instinct for the preferred soup.
Here are couched urchins, snugly comfortable
In the privilege of protection by Mayor Casasoprana.
Here is a mobile of squirlu nodding for crumbs
That escape from the squelched crust in your swimming fist.
They point, not exactly in the same direction,
But in a casual variety of angles that define
The distant point that may be in their thoughts,
Like an effort in perspective by Uccello.

The mind, moving over metres like the deity
Of the water's painted ceiling, a shadow in the light,
Makes of itself what it will: a blankness lulled
By recent waking, a contented sculling over
Dreamscape; or a beneficent enquiring spirit
Noting the plutonic shelving, the mossed gabbros
And eroded diorite, like ancient unwashed dishes,
And constructing a slow history of patient collapse
On this unchanging shore. Its only witness
Is the noise of waves, the planet's primal song,

The clamour of water frustrated at a threshold,
A plea of sorts, a luxurious performance.

You hear it all the time, behind all other sounds,
Even in sleep, when it is most like the voices
Which, if you could only manage to hear them,
Are ready to expound your deepest thoughts.
Put aside your calculations then,
Coast with the swell and dip, the sudden chill
Or warmth of the currents, the sound of your own breathing.
Let this pale otherworld lead you on and on
Through colder and bluer depths to some vision
Of an absolute, the dream-words still in the head
And hard to shake off, *comme de bien entendu.*

I will follow, as I always have done, and will do.
Of our many private performances, this is the freshest,
Our courses idly circling and meeting for a moment
In soundless acknowledgement. The sea stands for
Something that is always felt in the blood and breathing
Of our bodily lives. It is always in wait for us,
Pomme, for you are Pomme here, a little more carefree,
A bobbing, floating persona, concentrated in perception,
Full of your tenderest thoughts, Pomme, gazing out,
Graceful in water, striking from the shore,
Named by friends misreading your name in a letter,
Named in explicable error, callionymous Pomme.

And when the lightning begins to describe the mountains
With its startled flicker, the clouds are affronted,
The mistral blowing, the inky sea on horseback,
And we wonder what the fishes can find to do
As the gallons roll and split upon the bay.
The shutters, though shut, stutter through the night,
The wind shaking the house like an old box,
Not quite fooled into believing that it is empty.
It makes a bid to invade our secret dreams
Where we lie prone in great drama while the clock

Faithfully records the unnoticed times
Of these encounters with an alternative past.

Whatever the outcome of these broken narratives
Of wish and betrayal in the peopled inland
Of the mind, whatever the vexing forgottenness
Of their intriguing moods and premises,
We know that in the morning all will be still.
In the morning the sea will be whispering again:
'Pomme, Pomme!' After the storm, loosened weed
Is gathered in the rocks, the slim shoals feeding,
The sun stealthy over the eastern mountains,
Pebbles sharp in the light, and always the whispers:
'Pomme, Pomme!' And down you will go to the water,
The apple of my summer life.